FATTY LIVER
COOKBOOK

Over 100 Nutrient-Rich and Easy-to-Follow Recipes to Support Your Liver Health.
Includes a 4-Week Meal Plan.

Stefan Decker

Table of Contents

———— ❖ ————

Chapter 4: Soups and Salads 39

Chapter 5: Meat Dishes 50

INTRODUCTION

A Journey to Supporting Your Liver Health

---- ❖ ----

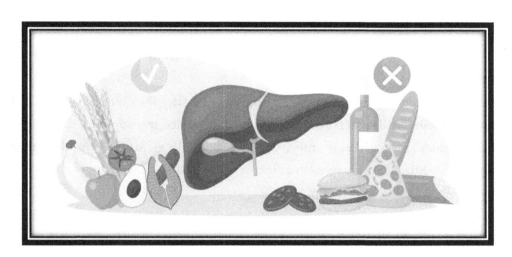

THE IMPORTANCE OF DIET FOR LIVER HEALTH

The Crucial Role of the Liver

The liver, a reddish-brown organ that weighs about three pounds, is located in the upper right part of the abdomen. It's an organ powerhouse, executing over 500 vital functions crucial for life maintenance. From filtering toxins out of the blood to supporting digestion and energy storage, the health of the liver is fundamentally important for overall well-being.

Fatty Liver

In recent years, the incidence of so-called fatty liver disease, characterized by excess fat stored in liver cells, has significantly increased. Often, it's a silent condition with few symptoms, yet it can have considerable impacts on health. Fatty liver can be categorized into two main types:

Alcoholic Fatty Liver Disease (AFLD): As the name suggests, this type is due to excessive alcohol consumption.

Non-Alcoholic Fatty Liver Disease (NAFLD): This type is not related to alcohol but is often linked with obesity and metabolic syndrome.

If left untreated, fatty liver disease can progress to more severe liver damage, such as inflammation, scarring and even liver failure.

Diet: The First Line of Defense

The good news is that diet plays a central role in the treatment and prevention of fatty liver diseases. What we eat has a direct impact on liver health. A diet high in refined sugars, saturated fats and processed foods can exacerbate fat accumulation in the liver. Conversely, a balanced diet rich in fibers, lean proteins and antioxidants can maintain liver health and prevent diseases.

The Healing Power of Nutrition

There is evidence that specific dietary changes can not only prevent fatty liver but also reverse it in its early stages. The liver possesses a remarkable ability to regenerate and heal, provided it is supplied with and cared for with the right nutrients. A diet including a variety of fruits, vegetables, whole grains and healthy fats can support liver function and promote the breakdown of excess liver fat.

Short Introduction to the Content of the Book and Its Objective

Welcome to the Fatty Liver Cookbook, a comprehensive guide designed to support you on your journey to optimal liver health through diet. This book is more than just a collection of recipes; it's a beacon of hope for those affected by fatty liver disease and a preventive measure for anyone wishing to maintain a healthy liver.

In this cookbook, you'll find a collection of recipes tailored to support liver health. Each recipe has been compiled with the following principles in mind:

Low in saturated fats and sugars: To prevent the accumulation of fat in liver cells.

Rich in fibers: To support digestion and the elimination of toxins.

Rich in antioxidants and nutrients: To provide the building blocks for liver repair and health.

But this book is more than a collection of recipes; it's a guide to understanding the importance of diet in maintaining a healthy liver. We delve into the scientific foundations of liver health, the specifics of a liver-friendly diet and how you can integrate these practices into your daily life.

Objectives of the Cookbook

The goals of this cookbook are multifaceted:

Educate: To impart fundamental information on how diet affects liver health, the consequences of fatty liver diseases and the power of food as medicine.

Nourish: It offers a selection of delicious, healthy recipes specifically tailored to the needs of a liver-conscious diet.

Empower: To equip you with the knowledge and tools needed to eat mindfully, thereby preventing or reversing fatty liver disease.

Inspire: We aim to encourage you towards a healthier lifestyle that extends beyond the kitchen, promoting well-being in all areas of life.

Support: We seek to create a sense of community and support for those dealing with liver health issues, so no one has to walk this path alone.

Content Overview

The Fatty Liver Cookbook is divided into several main sections, each serving a specific purpose in altering your diet and lifestyle:

Understanding Fatty Liver Disease: We start with a basic understanding of what fatty liver disease is, its types, causes and its impacts on overall health.

The Role of Diet in Liver Health: This section addresses how certain foods can worsen liver problems, while others support liver function and promote healing.

Principles of a Liver-Friendly Diet: Before we dive into the recipes, we establish the principles of a liver-friendly diet, including what to eat, what to avoid and why.

The Recipes: The heart of the book, this extensive collection of recipes has been carefully compiled to offer balanced, nutritious and tasty meals that align with a liver-friendly diet.

Tips for Planning and Preparing Meals: To help integrate these recipes into your life, this section offers practical advice on meal planning, grocery shopping and meal preparation.

Lifestyle Considerations: Since diet is just one aspect of health, this section offers advice on complementary lifestyle factors such as exercise, sleep and stress management.

Resources and Support: We provide additional resources for further education and support networks for people with fatty liver disease.

Your Journey to Liver Health

As you embark on this journey through our Fatty Liver Cookbook, remember that every meal is an opportunity to nourish and protect your liver. The path to better liver health begins on your plate and with each recipe, you take a step towards a healthier life.

The aim of this chapter is to give readers a clear understanding of the liver's importance, the impact of diet on liver health and the cookbook's task to guide them towards better eating habits.

Flipping through this cookbook, you will find more than just recipes; you'll learn how to craft a sustainable, liver-friendly lifestyle. The journey to better liver health is a marathon, not a sprint and this cookbook is designed to be a reliable companion at every step of that journey. Let's embark on this journey together, with the common goal of nurturing your liver, one meal at a time.

This introduction is designed to provide the reader with clear direction and elucidate what the book will offer. It creates a welcoming and informative narrative that emphasizes the significance of diet for liver health and the comprehensive nature of the cookbook.

Chapter 1: Principles of Liver Health and Well-being

Understand Fatty Liver and How Diet Can Help

In-depth Look at Fatty Liver: Causes, Effects and Prevention

Fatty liver, also known as hepatic steatosis, is a common condition characterized by the accumulation of excess fat in liver cells. While it's normal for the liver to contain some fat, a liver is considered fatty if more than 5 to 10% of its weight is fat. This condition is increasingly prevalent worldwide and is associated with a range of health problems.

Causes

The causes of fatty liver can be diverse and often interrelated, typically involving lifestyle factors and metabolic disorders. Here are the primary causes:

Metabolic Syndrome

Obesity: Especially central obesity, where fat accumulates around the waist.

Insulin resistance: A precursor to diabetes, where cells do not normally respond to insulin.

Hyperglycemia: High blood sugar levels, often associated with diabetes.

Dyslipidemia: Abnormal lipid levels in the blood, including high triglyceride levels and low High-Density Lipoprotein (HDL) cholesterol levels.

Diet

High consumption of refined sugars: Foods and beverages high in added sugar, particularly fructose, are linked to the accumulation of liver fat.

Excessive caloric intake: Leads to weight gain and obesity.

Genetic Factors

Certain genetic predispositions can increase the risk of developing fatty liver.

Other Causes

Rapid weight loss: Can cause fatty liver if weight loss is too rapid and unmonitored.

Certain medications: Such as corticosteroids, can contribute to fatty liver.

Toxins and alcohol: Excessive alcohol consumption is a well-known cause of liver fat accumulation, leading to alcoholic fatty liver disease.

Effects

A fatty liver disease can progress through several stages:

Simple fatty liver (steatosis): The first, non-inflammatory stage of fat accumulation.

Non-alcoholic steatohepatitis (NASH): A more severe form of fatty liver, where inflammation and liver cell damage occur.

Fibrosis: Scar tissue begins to replace healthy liver tissue.

Cirrhosis: The most severe stage, where liver function is significantly impaired, leading to liver failure or liver cancer.

The effects of fatty liver can thus range from mild, asymptomatic conditions to severe, life-threatening illnesses. It is also associated with an increased risk of cardiovascular diseases and type 2 diabetes.

Prevention

Lifestyle Changes

Healthy diet: Emphasizing whole grains, fruits, vegetables, lean protein and healthy fats.

Limiting sugar and refined carbohydrates: Especially reducing the intake of high-fructose foods.

Regular physical activity: Aiming for at least 150 minutes of moderate-intensity exercise per week.

Weight management: Achieving and maintaining a healthy weight through diet and exercise.

Medical Interventions

Medications: For treating comorbid conditions such as diabetes, hyperlipidemia and hypertension.

Regular screenings: For those at risk to monitor liver health and prevent disease progression.

Alcohol and Toxin Avoidance

Limiting alcohol consumption: To reduce liver strain.

Avoiding hepatotoxic medications and toxins: Including certain herbal supplements and environmental toxins.

Diagnostic Criteria

Diagnosing fatty liver typically requires a combination of medical history, blood tests, imaging and sometimes a liver biopsy:

Medical History and Physical Examination

Symptoms: Fatty liver is often asymptomatic but may present as fatigue or discomfort in the upper right quadrant.

Risk factors: Obesity, diabetes and high cholesterol in medical history.

Blood Tests

Liver enzymes: Elevated Alanine Aminotransferase (ALT) and Aspartate Aminotransferase (AST) levels can indicate liver inflammation.

Lipid profile: Dyslipidemia is commonly associated with fatty liver.

Imaging Studies

Ultrasound: A common first-choice diagnostic tool that can detect increased echogenicity of the liver indicating fatty liver.

CT and MRI: Can provide more detailed imaging and help quantify the amount of fat in the liver.

Transient Elastography (FibroScan): A non-invasive method to assess liver stiffness, which can indicate fibrosis.

Liver Biopsy

Considered the gold standard for diagnosing NASH and staging fibrosis. However, it is invasive and not routinely used for diagnosis due to its risks.

Treatment Options

The treatment of fatty liver focuses on eliminating underlying causes and preventing progression.

Lifestyle Interventions

Diet and exercise: The cornerstone of treatment, aimed at weight loss to reduce liver fat.

Nutritional counseling: To develop a tailored diet plan that reduces fat and sugar intake.

Pharmacotherapy

Vitamin E and Pioglitazone: Have been shown to improve liver histology in non-diabetic patients with NASH.

Metformin: Though not directly used to treat NASH, it can help manage diabetes and insulin resistance, thereby potentially reducing liver fat.

Statins: Can be safely used in patients with fatty liver to control dyslipidemia.

Bariatric Surgery

In selected cases, especially in individuals with significant obesity and comorbidities, bariatric surgery may be an option to achieve substantial weight loss and improve liver histology.

Emerging Therapies

New pharmacological agents targeting various aspects of NASH pathogenesis are currently under investigation. These include drugs that modulate lipid metabolism, insulin sensitivity, oxidative stress and inflammation.

Regular Monitoring

Regular follow-ups with liver function tests and imaging to monitor disease progression and the effectiveness of treatment measures.

Principles of a Balanced Diet for Liver Well-being

The liver is a vital organ responsible for numerous functions, including detoxification, protein synthesis and producing biochemistry necessary for digestion. A balanced diet is crucial for maintaining liver health and preventing diseases such as fatty liver, hepatitis and cirrhosis. This chapter describes the principles of a diet that supports liver well-being.

Nutrient Components of a Liver-Friendly Diet

Carbohydrates

Complex carbohydrates: Should form the basis of carbohydrate intake. Sources include whole grains, legumes and vegetables.
Fiber: Soluble fiber found in oats, fruits and vegetables helps regulate blood sugar levels and aids in weight control.

Proteins

Lean protein: Sources such as poultry, fish, tofu and legumes are preferred over red meat.
Low-fat dairy products: Options like skimmed milk and low-fat yogurt provide protein without excessive saturated fats.

Fats

Monounsaturated fats: Olive oil, avocados and nuts are good for liver health.
Polyunsaturated fats: Particularly omega-3 fatty acids found in fatty fish, flaxseed and walnuts support anti-inflammatory processes.

Vitamins

B-vitamins: Assist in metabolism and are found in whole grains, nuts and green leafy vegetables.
Vitamin E: An antioxidant that can help protect the liver from damage, found in nuts, seeds and green leafy vegetables.

Minerals

Zinc: Supports liver function and is found in nuts, seeds, dairy products and meat.
Iron: Should be consumed in moderation, as excess iron can be harmful to the liver.

Dietary Habits for Liver Health

Mediterranean Diet

This diet, rich in fruits, vegetables, whole grains, olive oil and fish, is associated with a lower risk of metabolic syndrome and fatty liver diseases.

DASH Diet

The DASH diet (Dietary Approaches to Stop Hypertension) includes low sodium, red meat and added sugars, which can positively affect blood pressure and liver health.

Plant-based Diet

Focuses on whole, minimally processed foods, reduces the intake of animal products and includes plenty of fibers that can benefit the liver.

Foods to Include

A liver-friendly diet includes a variety of foods that support liver function and protect against liver diseases. These foods provide essential nutrients, antioxidants, and compounds that support the liver's detoxification processes.

Fruits and Vegetables

Cruciferous vegetables: Broccoli, Brussels sprouts, cauliflower and kale contain glucosinolates that help the liver produce detoxifying enzymes.

Green leafy vegetables: Spinach, chard and mustard greens are rich in chlorophyll, which can aid the liver in neutralizing heavy metals and chemical toxins.

Berries: Blueberries, strawberries and raspberries are rich in antioxidants such as vitamin C and anthocyanins, which protect liver cells from damage.

Whole Grains

Fiber-rich grains: Oats, brown rice, barley and quinoa contain beta-glucans and are high in fiber, which can improve insulin sensitivity and aid in weight control.

Proteins

Plant-based proteins: Lentils, chickpeas and other legumes are excellent sources of protein and fiber, without the fat content of some animal proteins.
Fish: Especially those high in omega-3 fatty acids, such as salmon, mackerel and sardines, which have anti-inflammatory properties.

Healthy Fats

Nuts and seeds: Walnuts, flaxseeds and chia seeds are not only rich in omega-3 fatty acids but also provide vitamin E, a powerful antioxidant.

Avocados: They are rich in monounsaturated fats, which are heart-healthy and can help reduce liver inflammation.

Beverages

Coffee: Regular coffee consumption is associated with a lower risk of cirrhosis and liver cancer and can improve liver enzyme levels.

Green tea: Contains catechins, antioxidants that may aid in improving liver function and fat metabolism.

Herbs and Spices

Turmeric: Contains curcumin, known for its anti-inflammatory and antioxidant properties that can positively affect the liver.

Garlic: Rich in allicin and selenium, it can help activate liver enzymes that flush out toxins.

Fermented Foods

Yogurt and kefir: Provide probiotics that can improve gut health, with emerging evidence suggesting gut health is linked to liver health.

Sauerkraut and kimchi: Fermented vegetables that promote digestion and support liver function.

Superfoods

Beets: Contain nitrates and betalains, which have been shown to benefit heart health and reduce oxidative damage and inflammation in the liver.

Artichoke: Known for its effects on bile production and liver protection.

Incorporating a wide range of liver-friendly foods into your diet can have a profound impact on maintaining liver health and preventing diseases. These foods not only provide nutrients that support the liver's natural detoxification processes but also offer protection against oxidative stress and inflammation. As part of a balanced diet, these foods can contribute to optimizing liver function and complement other healthy lifestyle choices.

Foods to Avoid or Limit

While certain foods can promote liver health, others can be harmful and should be consumed in moderation or avoided altogether. These foods can exacerbate liver problems, contribute to the development of liver diseases or impair liver function overall.

Foods with a High Glycemic Index

Sugary snacks and beverages: Foods and drinks high in added sugar, such as sodas, candies and pastries, can lead to fat accumulation in the liver.

Refined carbohydrates: White bread, pasta and rice should be limited as they can contribute to weight gain and insulin resistance.

Saturated and Trans Fats

Fast food: Often contains many calories and trans fats, which can lead to obesity and liver damage.

Processed meats: Bacon, sausage and deli meats contain high levels of saturated fats and can promote inflammation.

Baked goods and packaged snacks: Cookies, cakes and chips often contain trans fats, which are harmful to the liver.

Alcohol

Alcoholic beverages: Excessive alcohol consumption can lead to a range of liver diseases, including alcoholic hepatitis, fatty liver and cirrhosis.

Sodium-rich Foods

Salty snacks: Chips and pretzels can contribute to fluid retention and high blood pressure.

Processed foods: Canned soups, frozen meals and ready-to-eat dishes typically contain high levels of sodium, which can worsen liver diseases by promoting fluid accumulation.

Certain Animal Proteins

Red meat: Contains high levels of saturated fatty acids and can contribute to liver fat accumulation, especially when consumed in large amounts.

Full-fat dairy products: Cheese and cream should be consumed in moderation due to their high saturated fat content.

Foods Containing Additives

Artificial sweeteners and preservatives: Some studies suggest they can have negative effects on liver health.

Artificial colors and flavors: These chemicals can unnecessarily burden the liver's detoxification process.

Fried Foods

Fried foods: Contain many calories and trans fats and can increase the risk of obesity and liver damage.

Salt: High salt intake can lead to fluid accumulation and increased blood pressure, exacerbating conditions like cirrhosis.

Raw or Undercooked Shellfish

Oysters and clams: Can harbor harmful viruses and bacteria that cause liver infections, especially in individuals with pre-existing liver diseases.

USE OF SUPPLEMENTS

Dietary supplements should be used with caution, as some can be harmful to the liver. Always consult your doctor before taking any new supplement.

While a balanced diet forms the foundation for a healthy liver, some people may need dietary supplements due to deficiencies or specific health conditions. However, since the liver processes everything we consume, caution must be exercised when taking supplements, as some can be hepatotoxic or impair liver function.

Understanding the Need for Supplements

Nutritional deficiencies: If a balanced diet cannot supply all the required nutrients - due to restrictions, allergies or particular health conditions - supplementation may be necessary.

Supporting the liver: Certain supplements are marketed for liver health or detoxification. While some may have positive effects, their efficacy and safety are not always scientifically proven.

Common Supplements for Liver Health

Milk thistle (Silymarin): Often used for its antioxidant properties to support liver health.

Vitamin E: Has shown promise in treating non-alcoholic steatohepatitis (NASH) but should be taken under medical supervision, especially at high doses.

Omega-3 fatty acids: May help reduce liver fat and inflammation in non-alcoholic fatty liver disease (NAFLD).

Zinc: Low zinc levels have been associated with liver diseases and supplementation could have beneficial effects.

Caution with Supplements

Potential toxicity: An excess of certain vitamins and minerals (e.g., iron and vitamin A) can damage the liver and even lead to liver injury.

Herbal supplements: Some herbal products can be contaminated with heavy metals or other substances toxic to the liver. Moreover, certain herbs can interact with medications and affect the activity of liver enzymes.

Unregulated market: Supplements are not as strictly regulated as medications and their efficacy and purity can vary.

Guidelines for Safe Use of Supplements

Medical supervision: Always consult a healthcare professional before starting any supplements, especially for those with liver issues or on medication.

Research: Look for supplements that have been clinically studied and proven safe.

Quality brands: Choose reputable brands whose ingredients have been independently verified (e.g., USP verified, NSF certified).

Appropriate dosage: Stick to recommended dosages and be cautious with high-dose supplements unless prescribed.

Interactions with Medications

Medication interactions: Some supplements can interfere with medications by either enhancing or weakening their effects. For example, St. John's Wort can decrease the effectiveness of many drugs, while vitamin K can affect the efficacy of blood thinners.

Liver metabolism: Since most medications are metabolized by the liver, any supplement that affects the activity of liver enzymes can alter the processing of medications.

Supplements can play a role in supporting liver health but must be used wisely and under professional guidance. A holistic approach that combines a balanced diet with lifestyle changes is the most effective strategy for maintaining liver health. In cases where supplements are deemed beneficial, choosing high-quality products and adhering to recommended dosages are crucial to avoid potential liver damage and ensure overall health.

MONITORING AND ADJUSTMENTS

Regular liver function tests can aid in adjusting the diet. Individual dietary needs can vary, especially with liver diseases, so a personalized diet plan should be developed in consultation with healthcare providers.

Continuous monitoring and regular adjustments are key components of maintaining liver health through diet. The liver's condition can change over time due to various factors such as diet, lifestyle changes and the natural aging process. Therefore, regular assessment and adjustment of dietary habits are crucial.

Regular Health Check-ups

Liver function tests: Blood tests such as ALT, AST, alkaline phosphatase and bilirubin levels provide insights into liver health.

Imaging: Ultrasound, CT or MRI scans may be recommended by a doctor to visualize the liver and detect fat accumulations, inflammation or fibrosis.

Nutritional Monitoring

Diet diary: Keeping a record of food and beverage intake can help identify areas for improvement and ensure a balanced nutrient intake.

Weight monitoring: Regularly tracking weight can help assess the effectiveness of a diet in maintaining a healthy weight, which is important for liver health.

Symptom Tracking

Well-being assessment: Monitoring energy levels, digestive health and overall well-being can indicate how diet affects liver health.

New symptoms: If symptoms such as jaundice, abdominal pain or chronic fatigue arise, consult a doctor immediately.

Dietary Adjustments

Nutrient intake: Adjusting the intake of macronutrients and micronutrients on medical advice, especially with changes in liver enzyme levels or symptoms.

Caloric intake: Caloric needs can change due to metabolism, activity level or liver health status and should be adjusted accordingly.

Lifestyle Modifications

Exercise: Regular physical activity should complement dietary efforts to maintain liver health.

Alcohol consumption: Depending on individual health status and in consultation with a doctor, alcohol intake should be limited or eliminated.

Re-evaluation of Supplements and Medications

Efficacy and necessity: Regularly review the need for ongoing supplementation, especially with changes in diet, health status or medication.

Interactions: Evaluate potential interactions between supplements, medications and dietary changes.

Personalized Nutrition

Tailored diets: Consult with dietitians or nutritionists for personalized dietary plans that consider individual health needs, preferences and cultural aspects.

Adjustment to health changes: As liver health improves or deteriorates, nutritional needs change and the diet should be adjusted accordingly.

Education and Support

Ongoing education: Stay informed through credible sources and healthcare providers about liver health and nutrition.

Support networks: Engage with support groups or nutritional counseling services for continuous support in dietary change.

Monitoring and adjusting a liver-healthy diet is a dynamic process that requires active involvement and regular communication with medical professionals. Individuals can significantly improve their liver health and function by continuously analyzing the efficacy of their diet and making appropriate adjustments. This proactive strategy allows for timely interventions that prevent liver problems and enhance overall well-being.

This chapter provides guidance for a balanced diet that supports liver function. Dietary requirements can vary greatly from person to person, especially among individuals with pre-existing health issues.

It's important to consult with healthcare professionals or nutritionists to create an individualized diet plan that meets your specific needs.

Chapter 2: Breakfast

Start Your Day with Nourishing, Liver-Friendly Choices

---- ❖ ----

1. Avocado and Egg Toast on Whole Grain Bread

Preparation Time: 10 min. | Cooking Time: 5 min. | Servings: 2 | Difficulty: Easy.

Ingredients:

- Whole grain bread: 4 slices
- Avocado: 1 medium
- Eggs: 2 large
- Olive oil: 1 tablespoon
- Lemon juice: 1 teaspoon
- Salt: 1/4 teaspoon
- Pepper: 1/8 teaspoon
- Cherry tomatoes (optional for garnishing): 1/4 cup
- Mixed leaf salad (optional for serving): 1/4 cup

Instructions:

Step 1: Halve the avocado, remove the pit, and scoop the flesh into a bowl.

Step 2: Add lemon juice, salt, and pepper to the avocado.

Step 3: Mash the ingredients with a fork until they reach the desired consistency.

Step 4: Preheat the oven to 180°C (356°F) or use a toaster.

Step 5: Lightly brush each slice of whole grain bread with olive oil.

Step 6: Toast the bread in the oven or toaster until crispy and golden brown, about 2-3 minutes.

Step 7: Heat a non-stick pan over medium heat.

Step 8: Crack the eggs into the pan and fry as desired: sunny-side up, over easy, or scrambled.

Step 9: Spread the mashed avocado evenly on the toasted bread slices.

Step 10: Gently place the cooked eggs on top of the avocado.

Step 11: If desired, garnish with cherry tomatoes and/or mixed leaf salad.

Step 12: Serve immediately and enjoy your avocado and egg toast warm and crispy!

Packed with nutrients, this toast is a wholesome choice for a quick meal. It supports liver health while providing delicious flavors and a satisfying texture.

Nutritional info (per serving): Cal 350 | Carb 30g | Fat 20g | Prot 12g | Fib 5g | Sugar 2g.

2. Oatmeal with Walnuts and Berries

Preparation Time: 5 min. | Cooking Time: 10 min. | Servings: 2 | Difficulty: Easy.

Ingredients:

- Oatmeal: 3/4 cup
- Water: 2 cups
- Milk (or any plant-based milk for a dairy-free option): 1 cup
- Walnuts, chopped: 1/4 cup
- Mixed berries (fresh or frozen, e.g., strawberries, blueberries, and raspberries): 1/2 cup
- Honey (or maple syrup for a vegan option): 2 tablespoons
- Ground cinnamon: 1/2 teaspoon
- Salt: a pinch

Instructions:

Step 1: In a medium-sized pot, bring the water and milk to a boil. Add a pinch of salt.

Step 2: Stir in the oatmeal and reduce the heat to simmer.

Step 3: Cook for about 10 minutes, stirring occasionally, until the oatmeal is soft and the mixture has thickened.

Step 4: Once the oatmeal is cooked, remove the pot from the heat.

Step 5: Stir in the ground cinnamon and half of the honey (or maple syrup). Mix well.

Step 6: While the oatmeal is cooking, prepare the berries. If using frozen berries, let them thaw slightly.

Step 7: Roughly chop the walnuts.

Step 8: Divide the oatmeal into bowls.

Step 9: Top each bowl with the chopped walnuts and berries.

Step 10: Drizzle the remaining honey (or maple syrup) over each serving.

Step 11: Serve warm and enjoy a cozy breakfast.

This oatmeal is a delightful mix of creamy textures and vibrant flavors. Packed with fiber, antioxidants, and healthy fats, it's perfect for liver health and a great start to the day.

Nutritional info (per serving): Cal 325 | Carb 45g | Fat 15g | Prot 8g | Fib 6g | Sugar 10g.

3. Quinoa Breakfast Bowl with Mixed Nuts and Seeds

Preparation Time: 5 min. | Cooking Time: 20 min. | Servings: 2 | Difficulty: Easy.

Ingredients:

- Quinoa: 1/2 cup
- Water: 2 cups
- Almond milk (or any other plant-based milk): 3/4 cup
- Mixed nuts (almonds, walnuts, hazelnuts), roughly chopped: 1/4 cup
- Mixed seeds (pumpkin seeds, sunflower seeds, chia seeds): 2 tablespoons
- Fresh fruit for garnishing (e.g., berries, banana slices): 1/2 cup
- Honey or maple syrup (optional, for sweetening): 2 tablespoons
- Salt: a pinch
- Ground cinnamon: 1/2 teaspoon

Instructions:

Step 1: Rinse the quinoa under cold water to remove the natural coating, saponin, which can make it taste bitter.

Step 2: In a medium-sized pot, combine the rinsed quinoa, water, and a pinch of salt.

Step 3: Bring to a boil, then reduce the heat to low, cover, and simmer for about 15 minutes, until the quinoa is tender and the water has been absorbed.

Step 4: Remove from the heat and let it stand covered for 5 minutes. Fluff with a fork.

Step 5: Add the almond milk and ground cinnamon to the cooked quinoa.

Step 6: Stir over medium heat until the mixture is hot and creamy, about 5 minutes.

Step 7: While the quinoa is cooking, chop the mixed nuts if not already done.

Step 8: Wash the fresh fruit and cut it into bite-sized pieces.

Step 9: Divide the warm quinoa mixture into two bowls.

Step 10: Sprinkle each bowl with the chopped nuts, mixed seeds, and fresh fruits.

Step 11: Drizzle with honey or maple syrup if desired.

Step 12: Serve immediately and enjoy your nutritious and filling breakfast bowl.

This quinoa bowl offers a perfect balance of protein, healthy fats, and slow-digesting carbs. It's a great way to fuel your body and support liver health.

Nutritional info (per serving): Cal 410 | Carb 52g | Fat 18g | Prot 12g | Fib 7g | Sugar 8g.

4. Spinach Mushroom Egg Muffins

Preparation Time: 10 min. | Cooking Time: 20 min. | Servings: 4 | Difficulty: Easy.

Ingredients:
- Eggs: 8 large
- Fresh spinach, roughly chopped: 4 cups
- Mushrooms, finely chopped: 1 cup
- Low-fat feta cheese, crumbled: 1/4 cup
- Olive oil for sautéing: 1 tablespoon
- Salt: 1/4 teaspoon
- Pepper: 1/8 teaspoon
- Cooking spray or olive oil for the muffin tin

Instructions:

Step 1: Preheat the oven to 180°C (356°F). Prepare a muffin tin by spraying with cooking spray or brushing with olive oil to prevent sticking.

Step 2: Heat the olive oil in a pan over medium heat.

Step 3: Add the chopped mushrooms and sauté for about 5 minutes until they release moisture and begin to brown.

Step 4: Add the chopped spinach and cook for another 2 minutes until the spinach has wilted.

Step 5: Season with salt and pepper, then remove from heat and let it cool slightly.

Step 6: In a large bowl, crack the eggs.

Step 7: Add the cooled spinach and mushroom mixture to the eggs. Add the crumbled feta cheese and stir.

Step 8: Evenly distribute the egg mixture across the muffin cups, filling each about three-quarters full.

Step 9: Bake in the preheated oven for 20 minutes, until the egg muffins are set and lightly golden on top.

Step 10: Let the muffins cool in the tin for a few minutes before removing them.

Step 11: Serve warm or allow to cool completely and store for a quick breakfast or snack.

These savory egg muffins are packed with nutrients and flavor. A convenient option, they are rich in protein and ideal for supporting liver health while staying delicious.

Nutritional info (per serving): Cal 200 | Carb 3g | Fat 14g | Prot 16g | Fib 1g | Sugar 1g.

5. Chia Seed Pudding with Kiwi and Coconut

Preparation Time: 15 min. | Cooking Time: 0 min. | Servings: 2 | Difficulty: Easy.

Ingredients:

- Chia seeds: 1/4 cup

- Coconut milk (light, for a lower-fat option): 1 2/3 cups

- Kiwi, peeled and sliced: 2 medium

- Honey or maple syrup (optional, for sweetening): 2 tablespoons

- Unsweetened coconut flakes, for garnishing: 2 tablespoons

- Vanilla extract: 1 teaspoon

Instructions:

Step 1: Mix chia seeds, coconut milk, and vanilla extract in a bowl. If desired, add honey or maple syrup for sweetness.

Step 2: Stir the mixture well to ensure the chia seeds are fully immersed in the liquid and can absorb it.

Step 3: Cover the bowl with a lid or plastic wrap and place it in the refrigerator overnight or for at least 6 hours to allow the chia seeds to achieve a pudding-like consistency.

Step 4: While the pudding is setting, peel and thinly slice or dice the kiwi, depending on your preference.

Step 5: Once the chia pudding has become firm and thick, stir it well to break up any clumps.

Step 6: Fill half of the pudding into two glasses or bowls.

Step 7: Layer a slice of kiwi on top of the pudding in each glass or bowl.

Step 8: Distribute the remaining pudding among the glasses and top with additional kiwi slices.

Step 9: Sprinkle the top of each pudding with coconut flakes to enhance texture and flavor.

Step 10: Serve immediately or keep in the refrigerator until ready to serve.

This refreshing chia pudding offers a creamy texture paired with the sweetness of kiwi and coconut. Rich in fiber and healthy fats, it's a nourishing choice to support liver health and keep you satisfied.

Nutritional info (per serving): Cal 300 | Carb 34g | Fat 18g | Prot 6g | Fib 9g | Sugar 10g.

6. Porridge Infused with Turmeric and Ginger

Preparation Time: 5 min. | Cooking Time: 15 min. | Servings: 2 | Difficulty: Easy.

Ingredients:

- Oats: 1 cup

- Water: 2 cups

- Fresh turmeric root, grated: 1 teaspoon

- Fresh ginger root, grated: 1 teaspoon

- Almond milk (or any other plant-based milk): 3/4 cup

- Honey or maple syrup (optional, for sweetening): 2 tablespoons

- Black pepper: a pinch

- Ground cinnamon: 1/2 teaspoon

- Salt: a pinch

Instructions:

Step 1: In a small bowl, mix the grated turmeric and ginger with a bit of almond milk (about 50 ml) to form a paste.

Step 2: In a medium-sized pot, bring the water to a boil.

Step 3: Add the oats along with the turmeric-ginger paste, ground cinnamon, and a pinch of salt.

Step 4: Reduce the heat to a simmer and cook for 10-15 minutes, stirring occasionally, until the oats are soft and the mixture has thickened.

Step 5: Once the oats are cooked and the porridge is thick, add the almond milk.

Step 6: Heat for another 2-3 minutes, stirring constantly. If you prefer a thinner porridge, add more milk as needed.

Step 7: Remove from heat and stir in honey or maple syrup to taste, if desired.

Step 8: Divide the porridge into bowls.

Step 9: Enhance the porridge with additional grated turmeric or ginger, a bit of cinnamon, or fresh fruit slices, if desired.

Step 10: Serve warm for a cozy and healthy breakfast.

This porridge is a warm, nourishing start to the day. Turmeric and ginger add anti-inflammatory benefits, making it a soothing choice for liver health.

Nutritional info (per serving): Cal 250 | Carb 45g | Fat 4g | Prot 6g | Fib 7g | Sugar 8g.

7. Baked Sweet Potatoes and Avocado Hash

Preparation Time: 15 min. | Cooking Time: 25 min. | Servings: 4 | Difficulty: Easy.

Ingredients:

- Sweet potatoes, peeled and cubed: 3 cups
- Avocado, cubed: 1 large
- Red bell pepper, cubed: 1 medium
- Red onion, finely chopped: 1 medium
- Olive oil: 2 tablespoons
- Garlic, chopped: 2 cloves
- Ground cumin: 1 teaspoon
- Paprika: 1 teaspoon
- Salt: 1/2 teaspoon
- Black pepper: 1/4 teaspoon
- Fresh coriander (optional, for garnishing): a small handful, chopped
- Lime: 1, cut into wedges for serving

Instructions:

Step 1: Preheat the oven to 200°C and line a large baking sheet with parchment paper.

Step 2: In a large bowl, mix the sweet potatoes, red bell pepper, and red onion.

Step 3: Combine the olive oil, chopped garlic, ground cumin, paprika, salt, and black pepper.

Step 4: Toss the vegetables with the oil and seasoning until they are evenly coated.

Step 5: Spread the vegetable mixture evenly on the prepared baking sheet.

Step 6: Bake for 25 minutes, turning halfway through, until the sweet potatoes are soft and slightly browned.

Step 7: Once the vegetables are baked, gently fold in the cubed avocado and fresh coriander, if using.

Step 8: Serve the hash warm, garnished with additional coriander and lime wedges on the side.

This dish brings together vibrant flavors and a satisfying mix of textures. Sweet potatoes and avocado provide fiber and healthy fats, making it a fantastic addition to a liver-friendly diet.

Nutritional info (per serving): Cal 280 | Carb 36g | Fat 15g | Prot 4g | Fib 8g | Sugar 5g.

8. Kale and Sweet Potato Breakfast Salad

Preparation Time: 15 min. | Cooking Time: 30 min. | Servings: 2 | Difficulty: Easy.

Ingredients:

- Sweet potatoes, peeled and cubed: 1 1/2 cups
- Kale, stems removed and leaves torn into bite-sized pieces: 4 cups
- Olive oil: 2 tablespoons for frying + 1 tablespoon for the dressing
- Eggs: 2 large
- Quinoa, rinsed: 1/4 cup
- Avocado, sliced: 1 medium
- Pumpkin seeds: 2 tablespoons
- Lemon juice: 1 tablespoon
- Honey (optional for the dressing): 1 teaspoon
- Salt: 1/2 teaspoon for seasoning
- Black pepper: 1/4 teaspoon for seasoning

Instructions:

Step 1: Preheat the oven to 200°C. Toss the cubed sweet potatoes with 2 tablespoons of olive oil, salt, and pepper.

Step 2: Spread the sweet potatoes on a baking sheet and roast for 25-30 minutes until tender and golden, turning halfway through.

Step 3: While the sweet potatoes are roasting, cook the quinoa according to package instructions. Combine 1 part quinoa with 2 parts water, bring to a boil, then simmer covered for 15 minutes until the water is absorbed. Fluff with a fork and set aside.

Step 4: In a large bowl, massage the kale with 1 tablespoon of olive oil and a pinch of salt until the leaves soften and wilt.

Step 5: Cook the eggs as desired: poached, fried, or boiled.

Step 6: In a small bowl, whisk together 1 tablespoon of olive oil, lemon juice, honey (if using), salt, and pepper to make the dressing.

Step 7: Add the roasted sweet potatoes, cooked quinoa, and sliced avocado to the bowl with the kale.

Step 8: Drizzle the dressing over the salad and gently toss to combine.

Step 9: Garnish the salad with a cooked egg and sprinkle with pumpkin seeds.

Step 10: Serve the salad immediately while the sweet potatoes are still warm.

This breakfast salad is a powerhouse of nutrients, blending warm sweet potatoes with fresh kale. The healthy fats and protein make it a perfect start to your day, supporting energy and liver health.

Nutritional info (per serving): Cal 450 | Carb 48g | Fat 25g | Prot 14g | Fib 10g | Sugar 6g.

9. Zucchini and Carrot Fritters

Preparation Time: 15 min. | Cooking Time: 10 min. | Servings: 4 | Difficulty: Easy.

Ingredients:

- Zucchini, grated: 1 1/2 cups
- Carrots, grated: 1 1/2 cups
- Eggs: 2 large
- Whole wheat flour (or chickpea flour for a gluten-free option): 1/4 cup
- Green onions, finely chopped: 2
- Garlic, chopped: 1 clove

- Olive oil: 2 tablespoons for frying
- Salt: 1/2 teaspoon
- Black pepper: 1/4 teaspoon
- Greek yogurt (optional, for serving): 1/2 cup

Instructions:

Step 1: Grate the zucchini and carrots. Place the grated vegetables in a clean kitchen towel or a sieve and squeeze out as much excess moisture as possible.

Step 2: In a large bowl, mix the squeezed zucchini and carrots, eggs, whole wheat flour (or chickpea flour), green onions, chopped garlic, salt, and pepper. Stir until well combined.

Step 3: Heat the olive oil in a large non-stick pan over medium heat.

Step 4: Using a heaped tablespoon, drop the mixture into the pan and lightly press down with the back of the spoon to form fritters.

Step 5: Fry for about 3-5 minutes on each side, until golden brown and cooked through.

Step 6: Serve the fritters hot, with Greek yogurt on the side for dipping, if desired.

These fritters are light, flavorful, and packed with vegetables. They are a versatile option for a quick meal or snack, supporting a liver-friendly diet while delighting your taste buds.

Nutritional info (per serving): Cal 180 | Carb 20g | Fat 9g | Prot 7g | Fib 3g | Sugar 4g.

10. Almond Butter and Banana on Sprouted Grain Toast

Preparation Time: 5 min. | Cooking Time: 0 min. | Servings: 2 | Difficulty: Easy.

Ingredients:

- Sprouted grain bread: 4 slices

- Almond butter: 4 tablespoons
- Banana, sliced: 1 large
- Chia seeds (optional, for garnishing): 1 teaspoon
- Honey (optional, for drizzling): 1 tablespoon
- Cinnamon (optional, for sprinkling): 1/2 teaspoon

Instructions:

Step 1: Toast the sprouted grain bread slices to your desired level of crispiness.

Step 2: Spread 1 tablespoon of almond butter evenly on each slice of toasted bread.

Step 3: Place banana slices on top of the almond butter on each slice of toast.

Step 4: If desired, sprinkle chia seeds and cinnamon over the banana slices to enhance the flavor and nutrients.

Step 5: Drizzle with honey for a touch of sweetness, if desired.

Step 6: Serve immediately as a quick, nutritious breakfast or snack.

This toast combines the creamy richness of almond butter with the natural sweetness of bananas. Packed with healthy fats and fiber, it's a simple yet energizing choice for your morning or afternoon.

Nutritional info (per serving): Cal 330 | Carb 36g | Fat 18g | Prot 10g | Fib 5g | Sugar 12g.

11. Spicy Breakfast Bowl with Lentils and Vegetables

Preparation Time: 10 min. | Cooking Time: 25 min. | Servings: 4 | Difficulty: Medium.

Ingredients:

- Green lentils, rinsed: 1 cup

- Olive oil: 2 tablespoons
- Garlic, chopped: 2 cloves
- Carrots, diced: 3/4 cup
- Zucchini, diced: 1 cup
- Red bell pepper, diced: 1 cup
- Spinach, roughly chopped: 4 cups
- Eggs: 4 large
- Water: 2 cups for cooking the lentils
- Salt: 1/2 teaspoon
- Black pepper: 1/4 teaspoon
- Paprika: 1/2 teaspoon for seasoning
- Fresh parsley: A handful, chopped for garnishing

Instructions:

Step 1: In a medium-sized pot, bring 500 ml of water to a boil. Add the rinsed lentils, reduce the heat to simmer, and cover.

Step 2: Cook the lentils for about 20 minutes until they are soft. Drain any excess water and set aside.

Step 3: While the lentils are cooking, heat the olive oil in a large pan over medium heat.

Step 4: Add the chopped garlic, carrots, zucchini, and red bell pepper to the pan. Sauté for about 5-7 minutes until the vegetables are soft.

Step 5: Stir in the spinach and cook for about 2 minutes until it wilts. Season with salt, pepper, and paprika.

Step 6: Once the lentils are cooked, add them to the pan with the vegetables. Stir well and season further if necessary.

Step 7: In another pan, cook the eggs to your preference: poached, fried, or scrambled.

Step 8: Divide the lentil-vegetable mixture among four bowls.

Step 9: Place a cooked egg on top of each bowl. Garnish with fresh parsley.

Step 10: Serve the breakfast bowls warm for a hearty and nutritious start to the day.

This breakfast bowl is loaded with protein, fiber, and vibrant vegetables. It's a flavorful way to energize your morning while supporting liver health with its nutrient-rich ingredients.

Nutritional info (per serving): Cal 300 | Carb 34g | Fat 10g | Prot 18g | Fib 9g | Sugar 6g.

12. Greek Yogurt with Nuts, Seeds and Honey

Preparation Time: 5 min. | Cooking Time: 0 min. | Servings: 2 | Difficulty: Easy.

Ingredients:

- Greek yogurt (low-fat or full-fat, according to preference): 1 3/4 cups
- Mixed nuts (almonds, walnuts, hazelnuts), roughly chopped: 1/4 cup
- Mixed seeds (pumpkin seeds, sunflower seeds, chia seeds): 2 tablespoons
- Honey: 2 tablespoons
- Fresh berries (optional, for garnishing): 1/2 cup

Instructions:

Step 1: If the mixed nuts are not pre-chopped, roughly chop them to make them easier to eat.

Step 2: Measure the mixed seeds and set aside.

Step 3: Divide the Greek yogurt into two bowls.

Step 4: Evenly distribute the chopped nuts and seeds over the yogurt in each bowl.

Step 5: Drizzle 1 tablespoon of honey over each bowl.

Step 6: If desired, garnish each bowl with fresh berries of your choice to enhance the flavor and nutrients.

Step 7: Serve immediately and enjoy your Greek yogurt bowl as a nutritious and filling breakfast or snack.

This Greek yogurt bowl is creamy, crunchy, and naturally sweetened. With its high protein content and healthy fats, it's perfect for boosting energy and supporting liver health.

Nutritional info (per serving): Cal 350 | Carb 30g | Fat 18g | Prot 20g | Fib 3g | Sugar 15g.

13. SMOKED SALMON AND AVOCADO WRAP

Preparation Time: 10 min. | Cooking Time: 0 min. | Servings: 2 | Difficulty: Easy.

Ingredients:
- Whole grain wraps: 2
- Smoked salmon: 3.5 oz
- Avocado, sliced: 1 medium
- Mixed leaf salad: 2 cups
- Cream cheese (low-fat, optional): 2 tablespoons
- Capers: 1 tablespoon
- Lemon juice: 1 teaspoon
- Fresh dill, chopped: a few sprigs
- Salt: a pinch
- Black pepper: a pinch

Instructions:
Step 1: Slice the avocado and drizzle with lemon juice to prevent browning.
Step 2: If using, lightly mix the cream cheese with chopped dill, salt, and pepper.
Step 3: Lay out the whole grain wraps on a clean surface.

Step 4: Evenly spread the dill cream cheese mixture on each wrap, leaving a small border around the edges.
Step 5: Arrange the smoked salmon slices on top of the cream cheese.
Step 6: Place the sliced avocado and a handful of mixed salad leaves on the salmon.
Step 7: Sprinkle capers over the filling.
Step 8: Carefully roll up the wraps, folding in the sides to enclose the filling.
Step 9: Cut each wrap diagonally in half and serve immediately or wrap in foil or parchment paper for a meal on the go.

This wrap combines the richness of smoked salmon with the creaminess of avocado, making it both delicious and nutritious. It's a quick, protein-packed option ideal for a liver-supporting diet.

Nutritional info (per serving): Cal 400 | Carb 33g | Fat 22g | Prot 20g | Fib 6g | Sugar 3g.

14. BAKED OATMEAL WITH PEAR AND WALNUT

Preparation Time: 10 min. | Cooking Time: 35 min. | Servings: 4 | Difficulty: Easy.

Ingredients:
- Oats: 2 cups
- Ripe pears, cored and sliced: 2 medium
- Walnuts, chopped: 1/2 cup
- Baking powder: 1 teaspoon
- Ground cinnamon: 1 teaspoon
- Salt: a pinch
- Milk (or any plant-based milk): 2 cups
- Egg: 1 large

- Vanilla extract: 1 teaspoon
- Honey or maple syrup: 3 tablespoons, plus extra for serving
- Butter or coconut oil (for greasing the baking dish): 1 tablespoon

Instructions:

Step 1: Preheat the oven to 180°C (356°F) and grease a medium-sized baking dish with butter or coconut oil.

Step 2: In a large bowl, mix the oats, chopped walnuts, baking powder, ground cinnamon, and a pinch of salt.

Step 3: In another bowl, whisk together the milk, egg, vanilla extract, and honey (or maple syrup) until well combined.

Step 4: Distribute half of the sliced pears at the bottom of the greased baking dish.

Step 5: Evenly spread the oat mixture over the pears.

Step 6: Pour the wet mixture over the oats, ensuring all oats are soaked.

Step 7: Top with the remaining pear slices and sprinkle with additional walnuts if desired.

Step 8: Bake in the preheated oven for 35 minutes, until the surface is golden brown and the oats are set.

Step 9: Let the baked oatmeal cool slightly before serving.

Step 10: Drizzle with additional honey or maple syrup if desired.

This warm and comforting baked oatmeal is perfect for a hearty breakfast. With natural sweetness from pears and the crunch of walnuts, it supports energy and liver health.

Nutritional info (per serving): Cal 450 | Carb 62g | Fat 18g | Prot 12g | Fib 8g | Sugar 18g.

15. CINNAMON APPLE QUINOA PORRIDGE

Preparation Time: 10 min. | Cooking Time: 15 min. | Servings: 2 | Difficulty: Easy.

Ingredients:

- Quinoa, rinsed: 1/2 cup
- Low-fat milk or unsweetened almond milk: 1 1/2 cups
- Apple, small, diced: 1
- Ground cinnamon: 1/2 teaspoon (plus extra for topping)
- Maple syrup: 1 tablespoon
- Chopped walnuts: 1 tablespoon

Instructions:

Step 1: Rinse the quinoa under cold water. In a saucepan, combine the rinsed quinoa with the milk and bring to a boil.

Step 2: Reduce the heat to low, cover, and simmer for 12-15 minutes until the quinoa is tender and the liquid is absorbed.

Step 3: While the quinoa cooks, dice the apple and toss it with ground cinnamon.

Step 4: Add the diced apple and maple syrup to the cooked quinoa, stirring gently to combine.

Step 5: Divide the quinoa porridge between two bowls and top with chopped walnuts and a sprinkle of additional cinnamon if desired.

Step 6: Serve warm and enjoy.

This cinnamon apple quinoa porridge is a warming and fiber-rich breakfast, packed with protein and healthy nutrients that support liver health.

Nutritional info (per serving): Cal 250 | Carb 38g | Fat 6g | Prot 8g | Fib 5g | Sugar 12g.

Chapter 3: Smoothie

Delicious and Nutrient-Rich Drinks for Liver Support

---- ❖ ----

16. Liver-Cleansing Green Smoothie

Preparation Time: 5 min. | Cooking Time: 0 min. | Servings: 2 | Difficulty: Easy.

Ingredients:

- Spinach, fresh: 2 cups

- Kale, stems removed, leaves chopped: 2 cups

- Apple, cored and diced: 1 medium

- Banana, peeled and sliced: 1 medium

- Lemon juice, freshly squeezed: 2 tablespoons

- Fresh ginger, grated: 1 teaspoon

- Water (or coconut water for added electrolytes): 1 cup

- Ground flaxseed: 1 tablespoon

- Ice cubes: a handful (optional, for a cooler smoothie)

Instructions:

Step 1: Thoroughly wash the spinach and kale leaves. Core and dice the apple. Peel and slice the banana. Grate the fresh ginger.

Step 2: Place the spinach, kale, apple, banana, lemon juice, grated ginger, water (or coconut water), and ground flaxseed into a blender.

Step 3: Add a handful of ice cubes if you prefer a cooler smoothie.

Step 4: Blend on high until smooth and creamy. If the smoothie is too thick, add more water until the desired consistency is reached.

Step 5: Pour the smoothie into two glasses and serve immediately to enjoy the full benefit of its nutrients.

This green smoothie is rich in antioxidants and essential nutrients that support liver cleansing. The blend of spinach, kale, and lemon is perfect for promoting overall liver health and detoxification.

Nutritional info (per serving): Cal 180 | Carb 39g | Fat 2g | Prot 5g | Fib 7g | Sugar 18g.

17. Golden Turmeric Smoothie

Preparation Time: 5 min. | Cooking Time: 0 min. | Servings: 2 | Difficulty: Easy.

Ingredients:

- Coconut milk (use light coconut milk for a lower-fat option): 1 cup

- Banana, peeled and sliced: 1 large

- Fresh turmeric root, grated (or ½ teaspoon ground turmeric): 1 teaspoon
- Fresh ginger root, grated: 1 teaspoon
- Ground cinnamon: 1/2 teaspoon
- Black pepper: a pinch
- Honey or maple syrup: 1 tablespoon (adjust according to desired sweetness)
- Ice cubes: a handful (optional, for a colder smoothie)

Instructions:

Step 1: Peel and slice the banana. Grate the fresh turmeric and ginger root. If using ground turmeric, measure the required amount.

Step 2: Place the coconut milk, banana, grated turmeric, grated ginger, ground cinnamon, black pepper, and honey or maple syrup into a blender.

Step 3: Add a handful of ice cubes if desired.

Step 4: Blend on the highest setting until the mixture is smooth and creamy. Adjust the sweetness if necessary by adding more honey or maple syrup.

Step 5: Pour the smoothie into glasses and serve immediately to enjoy its full benefits.

This golden smoothie is packed with anti-inflammatory ingredients like turmeric and ginger. A nourishing choice, it supports liver health and provides a refreshing boost to start your day.

Nutritional info (per serving): Cal 150 | Carb 24g | Fat 5g | Prot 2g | Fib 3g | Sugar 12g.

18. BERRY ANTIOXIDANT SMOOTHIE

Preparation Time: 5 min. | Cooking Time: 0 min. | Servings: 2 | Difficulty: Easy.

Ingredients:

- Mixed berries (fresh or frozen, e.g., strawberries, blueberries, raspberries): 1 1/2 cups
- Greek yogurt (low-fat): 3/4 cup
- Spinach, fresh: 2 cups
- Chia seeds: 2 tablespoons
- Almond milk (or any other plant-based milk): 1 cup
- Honey or maple syrup (optional, depending on taste): 1 tablespoon
- Ice cubes: a handful (optional, for a cooler smoothie)

Instructions:

Step 1: If using fresh berries, thoroughly wash them. If using frozen berries, measure the required amount.

Step 2: In a blender, combine the mixed berries, Greek yogurt, fresh spinach, chia seeds, almond milk, and honey or maple syrup if using.

Step 3: Add a handful of ice cubes if desired.

Step 4: Blend on the highest setting until smooth and creamy. If the smoothie is too thick, add a little more almond milk until the desired consistency is achieved.

Step 5: Pour the smoothie into glasses and serve immediately to maximize nutrient intake.

This vibrant smoothie is rich in antioxidants and fiber, making it an excellent choice for promoting liver health and overall vitality. Perfect for a refreshing and energizing start to your day.

Nutritional info (per serving): Cal 220 | Carb 34g | Fat 6g | Prot 10g | Fib 8g | Sugar 18g.

19. TROPICAL DETOX SMOOTHIE

Preparation Time: 5 min. | Cooking Time: 0 min. | Servings: 2 | Difficulty: Easy.

Ingredients:

- Pineapple, diced: 1 cup
- Mango, diced: 1 cup
- Banana, peeled and sliced: 1 medium
- Fresh spinach: 2 cups
- Coconut water: 1 cup
- Ground flaxseed: 2 tablespoons
- Lemon juice, freshly squeezed: 1 tablespoon
- Ice cubes: a handful (optional, for a cooler smoothie)

Instructions:

Step 1: Peel and dice the pineapple and mango.

Step 2: Peel and slice the banana.

Step 3: Place the pineapple, mango, banana, fresh spinach, coconut water, ground flaxseed, and lemon juice in a blender.

Step 4: Add a handful of ice cubes if you prefer a cooler smoothie.

Step 5: Blend on the highest setting until smooth and creamy.

Step 6: If the smoothie is too thick, add more coconut water until the desired consistency is reached.

Step 7: Pour the smoothie into glasses and serve immediately to enjoy the full nutritional value.

This tropical smoothie is a refreshing blend of fruits and greens. Packed with antioxidants and fiber, it supports detoxification and promotes liver health.

Nutritional info (per serving): Cal 210 | Carb 40g | Fat 5g | Prot 4g | Fib 6g | Sugar 28g.

20. Beet and Berry Liver Smoothie
Preparation Time: 10 min. | Cooking Time: 0 min. | Servings: 2 | Difficulty: Easy.

Ingredients:

- Beetroot, peeled and diced: 1 medium (about 1 cup)
- Mixed berries (fresh or frozen, e.g., strawberries, blueberries, raspberries): 1 cup
- Apple, cored and chopped: 1 medium (about 1 1/4 cups)
- Lemon juice, freshly squeezed: 2 tablespoons
- Water (or coconut water for added hydration): 1 cup
- Ground flaxseed: 2 tablespoons
- Honey or maple syrup (optional for sweetening): 1 tablespoon

Instructions:

Step 1: Peel and dice the beetroot.

Step 2: Core and chop the apple.

Step 3: If using fresh berries, wash them thoroughly.

Step 4: Place the chopped beetroot, mixed berries, chopped apple, lemon juice, water (or coconut water), ground flaxseed, and honey or maple syrup, if using, into a blender.

Step 5: Blend on the highest setting until the mixture is smooth and creamy.

Step 6: If the smoothie is too thick, add more water or coconut water until the desired consistency is reached.

Step 7: Pour the smoothie into glasses and serve immediately to maximize the nutrient content and freshness.

This vibrant smoothie is packed with antioxidants and fiber. Beetroot and berries work together to support liver health, making this a refreshing and nourishing choice.

Nutritional info (per serving): Cal 200 | Carb 40g | Fat 4g | Prot 5g | Fib 8g | Sugar 25g.

21. Avocado Green Tea Smoothie

Preparation Time: 5 min. | Cooking Time: 0 min. | Servings: 2 | Difficulty: Easy.

Ingredients:

- Ripe avocado, peeled and pitted: 1 medium (about 3/4 cup)
- Spinach, fresh: 2 cups
- Green tea, brewed and cooled: 1 cup
- Greek yogurt (low-fat): 1/2 cup
- Honey or maple syrup (optional for sweetening): 1 tablespoon
- Ice cubes: a handful (optional, for a cooler smoothie)

Instructions:

Step 1: Peel and pit the avocado.

Step 2: Measure the required amount of spinach.

Step 3: Brew the green tea and let it cool to room temperature.

Step 4: In a blender, combine the peeled avocado, fresh spinach, brewed green tea, Greek yogurt, and honey or maple syrup if using.

Step 5: Add a handful of ice cubes if you desire a cooler smoothie.

Step 6: Blend on the highest setting until smooth and creamy.

Step 7: If the smoothie is too thick, add a little more green tea until the desired consistency is reached.

Step 8: Pour the smoothie into glasses and serve immediately to fully enjoy its nutritional benefits.

This creamy smoothie blends the antioxidants of green tea with the healthy fats of avocado. It's a refreshing, nutrient-dense option that supports liver health and overall wellness.

Nutritional info (per serving): Cal 180 | Carb 15g | Fat 10g | Prot 6g | Fib 4g | Sugar 6g.

22. Carrot-Ginger Smoothie

Preparation Time: 5 min. | Cooking Time: 0 min. | Servings: 2 | Difficulty: Easy.

Ingredients:

- Carrots, peeled and diced: 2 medium (about 1 1/2 cups)
- Fresh ginger, peeled and grated: 1 tablespoon
- Banana, peeled and sliced: 1 medium
- Orange, peeled and segmented: 1 large (about 1 cup)
- Greek yogurt (low-fat): 1/2 cup
- Water: 1 cup
- Honey or maple syrup (optional for sweetening): 1 tablespoon
- Ice cubes: a handful (optional, for a cooler smoothie)

Instructions:

Step 1: Peel and chop the carrots.

Step 2: Peel and grate the fresh ginger.

Step 3: Peel and segment the orange.

Step 4: Peel and slice the banana.

Step 5: In a blender, combine the diced carrots, grated ginger, sliced banana, segmented orange, Greek yogurt, water, and honey or maple syrup if using.

Step 6: Add a handful of ice cubes if you prefer a cooler smoothie.

Step 7: Blend on the highest setting until smooth and creamy.

Step 8: If the smoothie is too thick, add more water until the desired consistency is achieved.

Step 9: Pour the smoothie into glasses and serve immediately to maximize its nutritional value.

This vibrant smoothie combines the sweetness of carrots and banana with the zest of ginger, making it refreshing and liver-friendly. Packed with vitamins, it's a great start to your day.

Nutritional info (per serving): Cal 150 | Carb 35g | Fat 1g | Prot 5g | Fib 6g | Sugar 22g.

23. Sweet Potato Pie Smoothie

Preparation Time: 10 min. | Cooking Time: 0 min. | Servings: 2 | Difficulty: Easy.

Ingredients:
- Sweet potato, cooked and cooled: 1 medium (about 3/4 cup)
- Banana, peeled and sliced: 1 medium
- Oats: 1/4 cup
- Ground cinnamon: 1 teaspoon
- Vanilla extract: 1 teaspoon
- Almond milk: 1 cup
- Honey or maple syrup (optional for sweetening): 1 tablespoon
- Ice cubes: a handful (optional, for a cooler smoothie)

Instructions:
Step 1: Cook and cool the sweet potato.
Step 2: Peel and slice the banana.
Step 3: Place the cooked and cooled sweet potato, sliced banana, oats, ground cinnamon, vanilla extract, almond milk, and honey or maple syrup if using, into a blender.
Step 4: Add a handful of ice cubes if you prefer a cooler smoothie.

Step 5: Blend on the highest setting until smooth and creamy.
Step 6: If the smoothie is too thick, add more almond milk until the desired consistency is reached.
Step 7: Pour the smoothie into glasses and serve immediately to fully enjoy its benefits.

This creamy smoothie offers the comforting flavors of sweet potato pie in a nutritious drink. Packed with fiber and essential vitamins, it's an excellent liver-friendly option to satisfy your cravings.

Nutritional info (per serving): Cal 250 | Carb 55g | Fat 3g | Prot 5g | Fib 7g | Sugar 20g.

24. Papaya Digestive Smoothie

Preparation Time: 5 min. | Cooking Time: 0 min. | Servings: 2 | Difficulty: Easy.

Ingredients:
- Papaya, peeled, seeded, and chopped: 1 small (about 1 1/4 cups)
- Greek yogurt (low-fat): 3/4 cup
- Fresh ginger, grated: 1 teaspoon
- Ground flaxseed: 2 tablespoons
- Honey or maple syrup (optional for sweetening): 1 tablespoon
- Water: 1 cup
- Ice cubes: a handful (optional, for a cooler smoothie)

Instructions:
Step 1: Peel, seed, and chop the papaya.
Step 2: Grate the fresh ginger.
Step 3: Place the chopped papaya, Greek yogurt, grated ginger, ground flaxseed, honey or maple syrup if using, and water in a blender.

Step 4: Add a handful of ice cubes if you prefer a cooler smoothie.

Step 5: Blend on the highest setting until smooth and creamy.

Step 6: If the smoothie is too thick, add more water until the desired consistency is achieved.

Step 7: Pour the smoothie into glasses and serve immediately to maximize its nutritional value.

This tropical smoothie combines papaya and ginger for a refreshing and gut-friendly drink. Rich in enzymes and fiber, it's perfect for supporting digestion and liver health.

Nutritional info (per serving): Cal 220 | Carb 40g | Fat 3g | Prot 10g | Fib 6g | Sugar 25g.

25. Chia Seed Omega Power Smoothie

Preparation Time: 5 min. | Cooking Time: 0 min. | Servings: 2 | Difficulty: Easy.

Ingredients:

- Chia seeds: 2 tablespoons
- Spinach, fresh: 2 cups
- Banana, peeled and sliced: 1 medium
- Greek yogurt (low-fat): 3/4 cup
- Almond milk: 1 cup
- Honey or maple syrup (optional for added sweetness): 1 tablespoon
- Ice cubes: a handful (optional, for a cooler smoothie)

Instructions:

Step 1: Measure the chia seeds.

Step 2: Thoroughly wash the fresh spinach.

Step 3: Peel and slice the banana.

Step 4: Put the chia seeds, fresh spinach, sliced banana, Greek yogurt, almond milk, and honey or maple syrup if using, into a blender.

Step 5: Add a handful of ice cubes if you prefer a cooler smoothie.

Step 6: Blend on the highest setting until smooth and creamy.

Step 7: If the smoothie is too thick, add more almond milk until the desired consistency is achieved.

Step 8: Pour the smoothie into glasses and serve immediately to fully enjoy its benefits.

Packed with chia seeds and spinach, this smoothie is a powerhouse of omega-3s and antioxidants. Perfect for boosting your energy while supporting liver health and overall wellness.

Nutritional info (per serving): Cal 250 | Carb 35g | Fat 7g | Prot 15g | Fib 8g | Sugar 14g.

26. Cucumber-Mint Refreshment Smoothie

Preparation Time: 5 min. | Cooking Time: 0 min. | Servings: 2 | Difficulty: Easy.

Ingredients:

- Cucumber, peeled and diced: 1 medium (about 1 1/2 cups)
- Fresh mint leaves: 1/4 cup
- Greek yogurt (low-fat): 3/4 cup
- Lime juice, freshly squeezed: 2 tablespoons
- Honey or maple syrup (optional for sweetening): 1 tablespoon
- Water: 1 cup
- Ice cubes: a handful (optional, for a cooler smoothie)

Instructions:

Step 1: Peel and chop the cucumber.

Step 2: Thoroughly wash the fresh mint leaves.

Step 3: Place the chopped cucumber, fresh mint leaves, Greek yogurt, lime juice, honey or maple syrup if using, and water into a blender.

Step 4: Add a handful of ice cubes if you prefer a cooler smoothie.

Step 5: Blend on the highest setting until smooth and creamy.

Step 6: If the smoothie is too thick, add more water until the desired consistency is achieved.

Step 7: Pour the smoothie into glasses and serve immediately to fully enjoy its nutritional benefits.

This cucumber-mint smoothie is light, refreshing, and hydrating. With its cooling properties, it's a perfect choice for supporting liver health and keeping you energized.

Nutritional info (per serving): Cal 120 | Carb 20g | Fat 1g | Prot 9g | Fib 2g | Sugar 10g.

27. Almond Butter Protein Kick Smoothie

Preparation Time: 5 min. | Cooking Time: 0 min. | Servings: 2 | Difficulty: Easy.

Ingredients:

- Almond butter: 2 tablespoons

- Banana, peeled and sliced: 1 medium

- Oatmeal: 1/4 cup

- Greek yogurt (low-fat): 3/4 cup

- Almond milk: 1 cup

- Honey or maple syrup (optional for sweetening): 1 tablespoon

- Ice cubes: a handful (optional, for a cooler smoothie)

Instructions:

Step 1: Measure the almond butter and oatmeal.

Step 2: Peel and slice the banana.

Step 3: Combine the almond butter, sliced banana, oatmeal, Greek yogurt, almond milk, and honey or maple syrup if using, in a blender.

Step 4: Add a handful of ice cubes if you prefer a cooler smoothie.

Step 5: Blend on the highest setting until smooth and creamy.

Step 6: If the smoothie is too thick, add more almond milk until the desired consistency is achieved.

Step 7: Pour the smoothie into glasses and serve immediately to fully enjoy its benefits.

This protein-packed smoothie combines creamy almond butter with the energy-boosting goodness of oats and yogurt. It's an excellent choice for a filling breakfast that supports liver health and keeps you fueled throughout the day.

Nutritional info (per serving): Cal 320 | Carb 35g | Fat 15g | Prot 15g | Fib 5g | Sugar 12g.

28. Spicy Lemon-Apple Smoothie

Preparation Time: 5 min. | Cooking Time: 0 min. | Servings: 2 | Difficulty: Easy.

Ingredients:

- Apple, cored and diced: 1 medium (about 1 1/2 cups)

- Lemon, peeled and seeded: 1 medium

- Fresh ginger, grated: 1 teaspoon

- Greek yogurt (low-fat): 3/4 cup

- Water: 1 cup

- Honey or maple syrup (optional for sweetening): 1 tablespoon
- Ice cubes: a handful (optional, for a cooler smoothie)

Instructions:

Step 1: Core and dice the apple.

Step 2: Peel and seed the lemon.

Step 3: Grate the fresh ginger.

Step 4: Place the chopped apple, peeled and seeded lemon, grated ginger, Greek yogurt, water, and honey or maple syrup (if using) into a blender.

Step 5: Add a handful of ice cubes if you prefer a cooler smoothie.

Step 6: Blend on the highest setting until smooth and creamy.

Step 7: If the smoothie is too thick, add more water until you reach the desired consistency.

Step 8: Pour the smoothie into glasses and serve immediately to enjoy its full nutritional benefits.

This tangy smoothie combines the zest of lemon with the warmth of ginger for a refreshing drink. Loaded with antioxidants and vitamin C, it supports liver health and boosts immunity.

Nutritional info (per serving): Cal 150 | Carb 30g | Fat 1g | Prot 6g | Fib 4g | Sugar 18g.

29. Pumpkin Spice Smoothie for the Liver

Preparation Time: 5 min. | Cooking Time: 0 min. | Servings: 2 | Difficulty: Easy.

Ingredients:

- Pumpkin puree: 2/3 cup
- Banana, peeled and sliced: 1 medium
- Greek yogurt (low-fat): 3/4 cup
- Ground cinnamon: 1 teaspoon
- Ground ginger: 1/2 teaspoon
- Ground nutmeg: 1/4 teaspoon
- Almond milk: 1 cup
- Honey or maple syrup (optional for sweetening): 1 tablespoon
- Ice cubes: a handful (optional, for a cooler smoothie)

Instructions:

Step 1: Measure the pumpkin puree.

Step 2: Peel and slice the banana.

Step 3: Combine the pumpkin puree, sliced banana, Greek yogurt, ground cinnamon, ground ginger, ground nutmeg, almond milk, and honey or maple syrup (if using) in a blender.

Step 4: Add a handful of ice cubes if you prefer a cooler smoothie.

Step 5: Blend on the highest setting until smooth and creamy.

Step 6: If the smoothie is too thick, add more almond milk until you reach the desired consistency.

Step 7: Pour the smoothie into glasses and serve immediately to enjoy its full benefits.

This creamy smoothie brings the comforting flavors of pumpkin spice into a nutritious drink. Packed with antioxidants and fiber, it's a delightful way to support liver health while indulging in seasonal tastes.

Nutritional info (per serving): Cal 220 | Carb 40g | Fat 3g | Prot 10g | Fib 6g | Sugar 18g.

30. Kiwi-Flaxseed Revitalization Smoothie

Preparation Time: 5 min. | Cooking Time: 0 min. | Servings: 2 | Difficulty: Easy.

Ingredients:

- Kiwi, peeled and sliced: 2 medium (about 1 1/2 cups)
- Ground flaxseed: 2 tablespoons
- Spinach, fresh: 2 cups
- Greek yogurt (low-fat): 3/4 cup
- Almond milk: 1 cup
- Honey or maple syrup (optional for added sweetness): 1 tablespoon
- Ice cubes: a handful (optional, for a cooler smoothie)

Instructions:

Step 1: Peel and slice the kiwis.

Step 2: Measure the ground flaxseeds.

Step 3: Thoroughly wash the fresh spinach.

Step 4: Combine the sliced kiwis, ground flaxseeds, fresh spinach, Greek yogurt, almond milk, and honey or maple syrup (if using) in a blender.

Step 5: Add a handful of ice cubes if you desire a cooler smoothie.

Step 6: Blend on the highest setting until smooth and creamy.

Step 7: If the smoothie is too thick, add more almond milk until you achieve the desired consistency.

Step 8: Pour the smoothie into glasses and serve immediately to fully enjoy its benefits.

This refreshing smoothie is packed with fiber, omega-3s, and antioxidants. Designed to support liver health, it also revitalizes your body with its nutrient-rich blend of kiwi and spinach.

Nutritional info (per serving): Cal 220 | Carb 35g | Fat 5g | Prot 10g | Fib 7g | Sugar 15g.

Chapter 4: Soups and Salads

Light and Healing Dishes Packed with Flavor

---❖---

31. Soothing Turmeric Chicken Soup

Preparation Time: 15 min. | Cooking Time: 30 min. | Servings: 4 | Difficulty: Medium.

Ingredients:

- Chicken breast, boneless and skinless, cubed: 14 oz
- Olive oil: 1 tablespoon
- Onion, diced: 1 medium (about 1 cup)
- Garlic, chopped: 3 cloves
- Carrot, diced: 2 medium (about 1 1/2 cups)
- Celery, diced: 2 stalks (about 1 1/4 cups)
- Turmeric powder: 1 teaspoon
- Ground ginger: 1/2 teaspoon
- Chicken broth: 4 cups
- Salt: to taste
- Black pepper: to taste
- Fresh parsley: for garnishing (optional)

Instructions:

Step 1: Cut the chicken breast into small pieces.

Step 2: Chop the onion, carrot, and celery.

Step 3: Chop the garlic.

Step 4: In a large pot, heat the olive oil over medium heat. Add the cubed chicken breast and cook for about 5 minutes until slightly browned.

Step 5: Add the chopped onion and garlic to the pot. Cook until the onion is translucent, about 3 minutes.

Step 6: Stir in the diced carrots and celery. Cook for another 5 minutes until they start to soften.

Step 7: Add the turmeric powder and ground ginger to the pot. Stir well to coat the ingredients evenly.

Step 8: Pour in the chicken broth and bring the soup to a boil.

Step 9: Reduce the heat and simmer for 15-20 minutes until the chicken is cooked through and the vegetables are tender.

Step 10: Season with salt and black pepper to taste.

Step 11: Ladle the soup into bowls and garnish with fresh parsley if desired.

Step 12: Serve hot and enjoy the comforting and soothing flavors.

This warm and nourishing soup combines the anti-inflammatory power of turmeric with tender chicken and hearty vegetables, making it perfect for supporting overall health and liver wellness.

Nutritional info (per serving): Cal 220 | Carb 10g | Fat 7g | Prot 25g | Fib 2g | Sugar 4g.

32. Liver Detox Broth

Preparation Time: 10 min. | Cooking Time: 1 hour | Servings: 4 | Difficulty: Medium.

Ingredients:

- Water: 2 liters
- Onion, chopped: 1 large (about 1 1/2 cups)
- Carrot, chopped: 2 medium (about 1 1/2 cups)
- Celery, chopped: 2 stalks (about 1 1/4 cups)
- Garlic, chopped: 4 cloves
- Turmeric root, peeled and grated: 1 small piece (about 1 tablespoon)
- Ginger root, peeled and grated: 1 small piece (about 1 tablespoon)
- Fresh parsley: a handful
- Bay leaves: 2
- Sea salt: 1 teaspoon or to taste
- Black pepper: 1/2 teaspoon or as preferred

Instructions:

Step 1: Peel and grate the turmeric and ginger roots.
Step 2: Chop the onion, carrot, and celery.
Step 3: Chop the garlic.
Step 4: Wash the fresh parsley thoroughly.
Step 5: In a large pot, combine the water, chopped onion, carrot, celery, chopped garlic, grated turmeric, grated ginger, fresh parsley, and bay leaves.
Step 6: Bring the mixture to a boil over high heat.
Step 7: Once boiling, reduce the heat to low and let the broth simmer gently for about 1 hour, uncovered, stirring occasionally.
Step 8: After simmering for 1 hour, remove the pot from the heat.
Step 9: Season the broth with sea salt and black pepper, adjusting to taste.
Step 10: Strain the broth through a fine-mesh sieve or a cheesecloth into another pot or container to remove the solid ingredients.
Step 11: Discard the solids and keep the clear broth.
Step 12: Serve the liver detox broth hot or let it cool down and store it in the refrigerator for up to 3 days.

This cleansing broth is packed with anti-inflammatory ingredients like turmeric and ginger. Its light, nourishing properties make it an excellent addition to a liver-friendly diet.

Nutritional info (per serving): Cal 20 | Carb 5g | Fat 0g | Prot 1g | Fib 1g | Sugar 2g.

33. Carrot Ginger Purée Soup

Preparation Time: 10 min. | Cooking Time: 25 min. | Servings: 4 | Difficulty: Medium.

Ingredients:

- Carrots, peeled and diced: 4 cups
- Onion, diced: 1 medium (about 1 cup)
- Garlic, chopped: 2 cloves
- Fresh ginger, grated: 1 tablespoon
- Vegetable broth: 4 cups
- Olive oil: 2 tablespoons
- Salt: 1 teaspoon or to taste
- Black pepper: 1/2 teaspoon or to taste
- Fresh parsley: for garnishing (optional)

Instructions:

Step 1: Peel and chop the carrots.
Step 2: Dice the onion and chop the garlic.
Step 3: Grate the fresh ginger.
Step 4: In a large pot, heat the olive oil over medium heat. Add the diced onion and chopped garlic. Cook until the onion is translucent, about 3-4 minutes.

Step 5: Add the diced carrots and grated ginger to the pot. Stir well to combine.

Step 6: Pour in the vegetable broth and bring the mixture to a boil.

Step 7: Reduce the heat to low, cover the pot, and let the soup simmer for about 20 minutes until the carrots are soft.

Step 8: Once the carrots are soft, remove the pot from the heat and let it cool slightly.

Step 9: Purée the soup using an immersion blender or in batches in a blender until smooth and creamy.

Step 10: If the soup is too thick, add more vegetable broth or water until the desired consistency is reached.

Step 11: Season the soup with salt and black pepper to taste.

Step 12: Serve the carrot ginger purée soup in bowls. Garnish with fresh parsley if desired.

This smooth and flavorful soup combines the natural sweetness of carrots with the warmth of ginger. Packed with nutrients and antioxidants, it's an excellent choice for a liver-friendly diet.

Nutritional info (per serving): Cal 120 | Carb 18g | Fat 5g | Prot 2g | Fib 4g | Sugar 8g.

34. Savory Lentil and Kale Soup

Preparation Time: 15 min. | Cooking Time: 40 min. | Servings: 4 | Difficulty: Medium.

Ingredients:

- Lentils, rinsed and drained: 1 cup
- Kale, destemmed and chopped: 4 cups
- Carrot, diced: 1 large (about 1 cup)
- Celery, diced: 2 stalks (about 1 1/4 cups)
- Onion, diced: 1 medium (about 1 cup)
- Garlic, chopped: 3 cloves
- Vegetable broth: 4 cups
- Olive oil: 2 tablespoons
- Bay leaves: 2
- Salt: 1 teaspoon or to taste
- Black pepper: 1/2 teaspoon or to preference
- Fresh parsley: for garnishing (optional)

Instructions:

Step 1: Rinse and drain the lentils.

Step 2: Destem and chop the kale.

Step 3: Dice the carrot and celery.

Step 4: Chop the onion and mince the garlic.

Step 5: In a large pot, heat the olive oil over medium heat. Add the chopped onion and garlic. Cook until the onion is translucent, about 3-4 minutes.

Step 6: Add the diced carrot and celery to the pot. Cook for another 5 minutes until they begin to soften.

Step 7: Stir in the rinsed lentils and chopped kale.

Step 8: Pour in the vegetable broth and add the bay leaves.

Step 9: Bring the soup to a boil, then reduce the heat to low. Cover and simmer for about 30 minutes until the lentils are tender.

Step 10: Once the lentils are tender, remove the bay leaves from the pot.

Step 11: Season the soup with salt and black pepper.

Step 12: Serve the savory lentil and kale soup in bowls. Garnish with fresh parsley if desired.

This hearty soup is rich in plant-based protein and fiber, offering a nutritious, liver-friendly meal. The combination of lentils and kale makes it both satisfying and health-supporting.

Nutritional info (per serving): Cal 250 | Carb 40g | Fat 5g | Prot 15g | Fib 12g | Sugar 6g.

35. Miso Vegetable Soup with Tofu

Preparation Time: 10 min. | Cooking Time: 20 min. | Servings: 4 | Difficulty: Medium.

Ingredients:

- Tofu, cubed: 7 oz
- Carrot, sliced: 1 large (about 1 cup)
- Celery, sliced: 2 stalks (about 1 1/4 cups)
- Onion, chopped: 1 medium (about 1 cup)
- Garlic, chopped: 2 cloves
- Ginger, grated: 1 tablespoon
- Vegetable broth: 4 cups
- Miso paste: 3 tablespoons
- Soy sauce: 2 tablespoons
- Green onions, thinly sliced: 2 (for garnish)
- Sesame seeds: 1 tablespoon (for garnish)
- Salt: to taste
- Black pepper: to taste

Instructions:

Step 1: Cube the tofu.

Step 2: Slice the carrot and celery.

Step 3: Chop the onion and garlic.

Step 4: Grate the ginger.

Step 5: In a large pot, heat a bit of oil over medium heat. Add the chopped onion, chopped garlic, and grated ginger. Sauté for about 2-3 minutes until fragrant.

Step 6: Add the sliced carrot and celery to the pot. Cook for another 5 minutes until slightly softened.

Step 7: Pour in the vegetable broth and bring to a simmer.

Step 8: Add the cubed tofu to the pot and let simmer for about 10 minutes, allowing the flavors to meld.

Step 9: In a small bowl, mix the miso paste with a few tablespoons of hot water until smooth.

Step 10: Stir the miso mixture and soy sauce into the soup. Continue to simmer for another 2-3 minutes.

Step 11: Season with salt and black pepper to taste.

Step 12: Ladle the miso vegetable soup into bowls.

Step 13: Garnish with sliced green onions and sesame seeds.

This miso vegetable soup is not only soothing and flavorful but also a rich source of plant-based protein. The tofu and miso paste contribute to a nutritious, liver-supporting dish that's both comforting and light.

Nutritional info (per serving): Cal 150 | Carb 10g | Fat 8g | Prot 10g | Fib 3g | Sugar 4g.

36. Spicy Pumpkin and Sweet Potato Soup

Preparation Time: 15 min. | Cooking Time: 40 min. | Servings: 4 | Difficulty: Medium.

Ingredients:

- Pumpkin, peeled and cubed: 4 cups
- Sweet potato, peeled and cubed: 2 cups
- Onion, chopped: 1 large (about 1 cup)
- Garlic, chopped: 3 cloves
- Vegetable broth: 4 cups
- Coconut milk: 3/4 cup
- Red chili flakes: 1 teaspoon (adjust to taste)
- Ground cumin: 1 teaspoon
- Ground coriander: 1 teaspoon
- Olive oil: 2 tablespoons
- Salt: to taste
- Black pepper: to taste
- Fresh coriander: for garnish (optional)

Instructions:

Step 1: Peel and cube the pumpkin and sweet potato.

Step 2: Chop the onion and garlic.

Step 3: In a large pot, heat the olive oil over medium heat. Add the chopped onion and garlic. Sauté for about 2-3 minutes until fragrant.

Step 4: Add the pumpkin and sweet potato cubes to the pot. Cook for another 5 minutes, stirring occasionally.

Step 5: Pour in the vegetable broth and bring to a boil.

Step 6: Reduce heat to low, cover, and simmer for about 25-30 minutes until the pumpkin and sweet potato are soft.

Step 7: Once the vegetables are soft, remove the pot from the heat.

Step 8: Puree the soup using an immersion blender or a regular blender until smooth. If using a regular blender, return the soup to the pot.

Step 9: Stir in the coconut milk, red chili flakes, ground cumin, and ground coriander.

Step 10: Season with salt and black pepper. Adjust the spices according to your preference.

Step 11: Serve the spicy pumpkin and sweet potato soup in bowls.

Step 12: Garnish with fresh coriander if desired.

This velvety soup combines the sweetness of pumpkin and sweet potato with a spicy kick, perfect for supporting liver health. The creamy coconut milk balances the heat, making this soup comforting and nourishing.

Nutritional info (per serving): Cal 200 | Carb 30g | Fat 8g | Prot 4g | Fib 5g | Sugar 12g.

37. Beetroot and Cabbage Healing Soup

Preparation Time: 15 mins | Cooking Time: 30 mins | Servings: 4 | Difficulty: Easy.

Ingredients:

- Beetroot, peeled and cubed: 2 cups
- Cabbage, shredded: 4 cups
- Carrot, sliced: 1 large (about 1 cup)
- Onion, chopped: 1 medium (about 1 cup)
- Garlic, chopped: 2 cloves
- Vegetable broth: 4 cups
- Olive oil: 2 tablespoons
- Apple cider vinegar: 2 tablespoons
- Fresh dill: 2 tablespoons (for garnish)
- Salt: to taste
- Black pepper: to taste

Instructions:

Step 1: Peel and cube the beetroot.

Step 2: Shred the cabbage.

Step 3: Slice the carrot and chop the onion.

Step 4: Chop the garlic.

Step 5: In a large pot, heat the olive oil over medium heat. Add the chopped onion and garlic. Sauté until soft, about 2-3 minutes.

Step 6: Add the cubed beetroot, shredded cabbage, and sliced carrot to the pot. Cook for another 5 minutes, stirring occasionally.

Step 7: Pour in the vegetable broth and bring to a simmer.

Step 8: Cover and cook for about 20 minutes until the vegetables are soft.

Step 9: Stir in apple cider vinegar, salt, and black pepper to taste. Adjust the seasoning as preferred.

Step 10: Ladle the beetroot and cabbage healing soup into bowls.

Step 11: Garnish with fresh dill.

This vibrant and nourishing soup combines the earthy flavors of beetroot and cabbage with the tang of apple cider vinegar, making it a powerful addition to a liver-supporting diet.

Nutritional info (per serving): Cal 120 | Carb 20g | Fat 4g | Prot 3g | Fib 6g | Sugar 9g.

38. LIVER-SUPPORTING SALAD WITH BRAZIL NUTS

Preparation Time: 15 min. | Cooking Time: 30 min. | Servings: 4 | Difficulty: Medium.

Ingredients:
- Spinach: 5 cups
- Kale, stems removed and chopped: 5 cups
- Beetroot, grated: 1 medium (about 1 cup)
- Carrot, grated: 1 medium (about 3/4 cup)
- Red cabbage, shredded: 1 cup
- Brazil nuts, chopped: 1/3 cup
- Lemon, juiced: 1
- Extra virgin olive oil: 2 tablespoons
- Salt: to taste
- Black pepper: to taste

Instructions:
Step 1: Thoroughly wash and pat dry the spinach and kale. Tear the spinach into bite-sized pieces.

Step 2: Remove the stems from the kale leaves and finely chop them.

Step 3: Grate the beetroot and carrot.

Step 4: Shred the red cabbage.

Step 5: Place all the prepared vegetables in a large bowl.

Step 6: Add the chopped Brazil nuts to the bowl with the vegetables.

Step 7: Drizzle the salad with freshly squeezed lemon juice and extra virgin olive oil.

Step 8: Season with salt and black pepper to taste.

Step 9: Gently toss the salad to mix all the ingredients and coat them evenly with the dressing.

Step 10: Divide the salad into two portions and serve immediately.

This nutrient-packed salad is full of liver-supporting ingredients, such as kale, beetroot, and Brazil nuts. It's a refreshing and healthy choice to nourish your body while supporting liver detoxification.

Nutritional info (per serving): Cal 250 | Carb 20g | Fat 18g | Prot 8g | Fib 6g | Sugar 10g.

39. QUINOA AND ROASTED VEGETABLE SALAD

Preparation Time: 15 min. | Cooking Time: 25 min. | Servings: 4 | Difficulty: Easy.

Ingredients:
- Quinoa: 1 cup
- Bell peppers, diced: 2 medium (about 2 cups)
- Zucchini, diced: 1 medium (about 1 1/2 cups)
- Red onion, sliced: 1 medium (about 1 cup)
- Cherry tomatoes: 1 1/2 cups
- Olive oil: 3 tablespoons
- Balsamic vinegar: 2 tablespoons
- Garlic, chopped: 2 cloves
- Salt: to taste
- Black pepper: to taste

- Fresh parsley, chopped: 2 tablespoons (for garnishing)

Instructions:

Step 1: Preheat the oven to 200°C (400°F).

Step 2: Rinse the quinoa in a fine mesh strainer under cold water.

Step 3: In a pot, combine the rinsed quinoa with 400ml of water.

Step 4: Bring to a boil, then reduce the heat and simmer covered for about 15 minutes until the quinoa is tender and the water has been absorbed.

Step 5: Remove from heat and let it sit covered for 5 minutes.

Step 6: Fluff with a fork.

Step 7: On a large baking sheet, mix the diced bell peppers, zucchini, sliced red onions, and cherry tomatoes with olive oil, balsamic vinegar, chopped garlic, salt, and black pepper until evenly coated.

Step 8: Spread the vegetables in an even layer on the baking sheet.

Step 9: Roast in the preheated oven for about 20-25 minutes, stirring halfway through, until the vegetables are tender and slightly caramelized.

Step 10: In a large bowl, mix the cooked quinoa with the roasted vegetables.

Step 11: Adjust seasoning with salt and black pepper if necessary.

Step 12: Serve the quinoa and roasted vegetable salad on serving plates or bowls.

Step 13: Garnish with chopped fresh parsley. Serve warm or at room temperature.

This colorful salad combines the rich flavors of roasted vegetables with the nutritious goodness of quinoa. It's a perfect dish for liver health, offering fiber and antioxidants in every bite.

Nutritional info (per serving): Cal 280 | Carb 40g | Fat 10g | Prot 8g | Fib 6g | Sugar 12g.

40. AVOCADO AND GRAPEFRUIT SALAD

Preparation Time: 15 min. | Cooking Time: 0 min. | Servings: 2 | Difficulty: Easy.

Ingredients:

- Ripe avocado, diced: 1 large (about 1 cup)
- Grapefruit, segmented: 1 large
- Mixed greens: 4 cups
- Red onion, thinly sliced: 1/4 small (about 2 tablespoons)
- Olive oil: 2 tablespoons
- Lemon juice: 1 tablespoon
- Honey: 1 teaspoon
- Salt: to taste
- Black pepper: to taste
- Roasted walnuts, chopped: 1/4 cup (for garnishing)
- Fresh parsley, chopped: 2 tablespoons (for garnishing)

Instructions:

Step 1: In a small bowl, whisk together olive oil, lemon juice, honey, salt, and black pepper until well combined. Set aside.

Step 2: In a large bowl, mix the mixed greens with the diced avocado and segmented grapefruit.

Step 3: Add the thinly sliced red onion to the bowl.

Step 4: Drizzle the prepared dressing over the salad mixture.

Step 5: Gently toss the salad until it is evenly coated with the dressing.

Step 6: Evenly distribute the salad onto two serving plates.

Step 7: Garnish with chopped roasted walnuts and fresh parsley.

Step 8: Serve immediately to enjoy the fresh flavors.

This refreshing salad combines the creamy texture of avocado with the citrusy tang of grapefruit, offering a vibrant, liver-friendly dish packed with healthy fats and nutrients.

Nutritional info (per serving): Cal 280 | Carb 22g | Fat 20g | Prot 4g | Fib 8g | Sugar 12g.

41. KALE, APPLE AND WALNUT SALAD

Preparation Time: 15 min. | Cooking Time: 0 min. | Servings: 2 | Difficulty: Easy.

Ingredients:

- Kale, stems removed and leaves torn into bite-sized pieces: 5 cups
- Apple, thinly sliced: 1 medium (about 1 1/2 cups)
- Walnuts, coarsely chopped: 1/2 cup
- Red onion, thinly sliced: 1/4 small (about 2 tablespoons)
- Lemon juice: 2 tablespoons
- Olive oil: 2 tablespoons
- Honey: 1 tablespoon
- Salt: to taste
- Black pepper: to taste

Instructions:

Step 1: In a small bowl, whisk together lemon juice, olive oil, honey, salt, and black pepper until well combined. Set aside.

Step 2: Place the torn kale leaves into a large mixing bowl.

Step 3: Drizzle half of the prepared dressing over the kale.

Step 4: Massage the kale leaves with your hands for 2 to 3 minutes until they start to soften and wilt.

Step 5: Add the thinly sliced apple, chopped walnuts, and sliced red onion to the bowl with the massaged kale.

Step 6: Drizzle the remaining dressing over the salad ingredients.

Step 7: Gently toss the salad until all the ingredients are evenly coated with the dressing.

Step 8: Evenly distribute the salad onto two serving plates.

Step 9: Serve immediately and enjoy this healthy, vibrant salad.

This energizing salad combines the richness of kale, the sweetness of apple, and the crunch of walnuts, making it an excellent choice for a liver-supporting meal.

Nutritional info (per serving): Cal 270 | Carb 25g | Fat 18g | Prot 5g | Fib 6g | Sugar 14g.

42. BEETROOT AND ARUGULA SALAD

Preparation Time: 15 min. | Cooking Time: 40 min. | Servings: 2 | Difficulty: Easy.

Ingredients:

- Beetroots, peeled and thinly sliced: 2 medium (about 2 cups)
- Arugula: 4 cups
- Goat cheese, crumbled: 1/4 cup
- Walnuts, coarsely chopped: 1/4 cup
- Balsamic vinegar: 2 tablespoons
- Olive oil: 2 tablespoons
- Salt: to taste
- Black pepper: to taste

Instructions:

Step 1: Preheat the oven to 200°C (400°F).

Step 2: Place the thinly sliced beetroots on a baking tray lined with parchment paper.

Step 3: Drizzle with olive oil, season with salt and pepper, and toss to ensure they are evenly coated.

Step 4: Roast in the preheated oven for about 30-40 minutes or until soft when pierced with a fork.

Step 5: Remove from the oven and allow to cool slightly.

Step 6: In a small bowl, whisk together balsamic vinegar, olive oil, salt, and black pepper to make the dressing.

Step 7: In a large bowl, mix the roasted beetroot slices and arugula.

Step 8: Drizzle the dressing over the salad and gently toss to coat.

Step 9: Sprinkle the salad with crumbled goat cheese and chopped walnuts. Evenly divide the salad onto two serving plates.

This vibrant salad combines the earthy flavor of roasted beetroot with the peppery bite of arugula, topped with the richness of goat cheese and the crunch of walnuts, offering a nourishing dish full of antioxidants.

Nutritional info (per serving): Cal 250 | Carb 19g | Fat 17g | Prot 7g | Fib 5g | Sugar 10g.

43. Broccoli and Mixed Berries Detox Salad

Preparation Time: 15 min. | Cooking Time: 0 min. | Servings: 2 | Difficulty: Easy.

Ingredients:
- Broccoli, florets cut into bite-sized pieces: 2 cups
- Mixed berries (e.g., strawberries, blueberries, raspberries): 1/2 cup
- Red onion, thinly sliced: 1/4 small (about 2 tablespoons)
- Almonds, sliced: 1/4 cup
- Fresh parsley, chopped: 2 tablespoons
For the Dressing:
- Olive oil: 2 tablespoons
- Lemon juice: 1 tablespoon
- Dijon mustard: 1 teaspoon
- Honey or maple syrup: 1 teaspoon
- Salt: to taste
- Black pepper: to preference

Instructions:
Step 1: Rinse the broccoli florets under cold water and pat dry with a kitchen towel.

Step 2: Cut the broccoli into bite-sized florets.

Step 3: In a large bowl, mix the broccoli florets, mixed berries, thinly sliced red onion, sliced almonds, and chopped parsley.

Step 4: In a small bowl, whisk together olive oil, lemon juice, Dijon mustard, honey or maple syrup, salt, and black pepper until well combined.

Step 5: Drizzle the dressing over the salad ingredients in the mixing bowl.

Step 6: Gently toss the salad to ensure all ingredients are evenly coated with the dressing.

Step 7: Divide the salad into two bowls.

This detox salad is a fresh and vibrant combination of nutritious broccoli, antioxidant-rich berries, and crunchy almonds, making it a perfect choice for a refreshing liver-friendly meal.

Nutritional info (per serving): Cal 180 | Carb 16g | Fat 12g | Prot 5g | Fib 5g | Sugar 9g.

44. Spicy Chickpea and Cucumber Salad

Preparation Time: 15 min. | Cooking Time: 0 min. | Servings: 2 | Difficulty: Easy.

Ingredients:

- Canned chickpeas, drained and rinsed: 1 cup
- Cucumber, diced: 1 medium
- Cherry tomatoes, halved: 1/2 cup
- Red onion, thinly sliced: 1/4 small (about 2 tablespoons)
- Fresh coriander (cilantro), chopped: 2 tablespoons
- Jalapeno pepper, thinly sliced: 1 (remove seeds for less heat)

For the Dressing:
- Olive oil: 2 tablespoons
- Lemon juice: 1 tablespoon
- Ground cumin: 1/2 teaspoon
- Chili powder: 1/2 teaspoon
- Salt: to taste
- Black pepper: to preference

Instructions:

Step 1: In a large bowl, mix the drained and rinsed chickpeas, diced cucumber, halved cherry tomatoes, thinly sliced red onion, chopped cilantro, and thinly sliced jalapeno pepper.

Step 2: In a small bowl, whisk together olive oil, lemon juice, ground cumin, chili powder, salt, and black pepper until well combined.

Step 3: Drizzle the dressing over the salad ingredients in the mixing bowl.

Step 4: Gently toss the salad to ensure all ingredients are evenly coated with the dressing.

Step 5: Divide the salad into two bowls.

This refreshing and spicy salad combines chickpeas, crunchy vegetables, and a zesty dressing that packs flavor and supports liver health with its antioxidants and healthy fats.

Nutritional info (per serving): Cal 220 | Carb 28g | Fat 10g | Prot 7g | Fib 6g | Sugar 7g.

45. Sweet Potato and Spinach Salad

Preparation Time: 15 min. | Cooking Time: 0 min. | Servings: 2 | Difficulty: Easy.

Ingredients:

- Sweet potatoes, peeled and diced: 2 medium (about 3 cups)
- Baby spinach: 4 cups
- Red onion, thinly sliced: 1/4 small (about 2 tablespoons)
- Cherry tomatoes, halved: 1 cup
- Avocado, diced: 1 medium
- Feta cheese, crumbled (optional): 1/2 cup
- Pumpkin seeds: 2 tablespoons

For the Dressing:
- Olive oil: 3 tablespoons
- Balsamic vinegar: 1 tablespoon
- Dijon mustard: 1 teaspoon
- Honey (optional, or replace with a sugar-free sweetener): 1 teaspoon
- Salt and pepper: to taste

Instructions:

Step 1: Preheat the oven to 400°F (200°C).

Step 2: Toss the diced sweet potatoes on a baking sheet lined with parchment paper with 1 tablespoon of olive oil, season with salt and pepper.

Step 3: Roast for 20 minutes, until soft and slightly caramelized.

Step 4: In a large salad bowl, mix the baby spinach, thinly sliced red onions, halved cherry tomatoes, and diced avocado.

Step 5: Once the sweet potatoes are roasted and slightly cooled, add them to the salad.

Step 6: In a small bowl, whisk together the remaining olive oil, balsamic vinegar, Dijon mustard, and honey.

Step 7: Season the dressing with salt and pepper.

Step 8: Drizzle the dressing over the salad and gently toss to combine.

Step 9: Sprinkle the salad with crumbled feta cheese (if using) and pumpkin seeds before serving.

This vibrant salad brings together roasted sweet potatoes and creamy avocado, creating a comforting dish full of healthy fats and fiber. It's a nourishing option that supports liver health while offering a delicious balance of flavors.

Nutritional info (per serving): Cal 380 | Carb 38g | Fat 22g | Prot 8g | Fib 7g | Sugar 10g.

Chapter 5: Meat Dishes

Wholesome and Protein-Packed Recipes for Your Liver

❖

46. Grilled Chicken and Avocado Salad

Preparation Time: 15 min. | Cooking Time: 15 min. | Servings: 2 | Difficulty: Easy.

Ingredients:

- Chicken breasts, boneless and skinless: 2 (about 10.5 oz)
- Mixed leaf salad: 6 cups
- Cherry tomatoes, halved: 1 cup
- Avocado, sliced: 1 medium
- Red onion, thinly sliced: 1/4 small (about 2 tablespoons)
- Cucumber, sliced: 1/2 medium
- Olive oil: 2 tablespoons
- Lemon juice: 1 tablespoon
- Garlic, chopped: 1 clove
- Salt: to taste
- Black pepper: to taste

Instructions:

Step 1: Preheat a grill or grill pan over medium to high heat.

Step 2: Season the chicken breasts with salt and black pepper.

Step 3: Grill the chicken breasts for about 6-7 minutes per side, until they are cooked through and no longer pink in the middle.

Step 4: Remove the chicken from the grill and let it rest for a few minutes before slicing.

Step 5: In a large bowl, mix the mixed leaf salad, halved cherry tomatoes, sliced avocado, thinly sliced red onion, and sliced cucumber.

Step 6: In a small bowl, whisk together the olive oil, lemon juice, chopped garlic, salt, and black pepper until well combined.

Step 7: Add the sliced grilled chicken to the bowl with the salad ingredients.

Step 8: Drizzle the dressing over the salad.

Step 9: Gently toss the salad until all ingredients are evenly coated with the dressing.

Step 10: Divide the salad onto two serving plates.

This fresh and protein-packed salad combines the richness of avocado with the lightness of grilled chicken. A perfect choice for a healthy, liver-supporting meal.

Nutritional info (per serving): Cal 380 | Carb 12g | Fat 20g | Prot 35g | Fib 5g | Sugar 2g.

47. Turkey-Quinoa Meatballs with Tomato-Basil Sauce

Preparation Time: 20 min. | Cooking Time: 25 min. | Servings: 4 | Difficulty: Medium.

Ingredients:

For the Meatballs:

- Lean turkey mince: 1 lb
- Cooked quinoa: 1 cup
- Onion, finely chopped: 1 small (about 1/2 cup)
- Garlic, chopped: 2 cloves
- Fresh parsley, chopped: 2 tablespoons
- Egg: 1 large
- Salt: 1 teaspoon
- Black pepper: 1/2 teaspoon
- Olive oil: 1 tablespoon (for cooking)

For the Tomato-Basil Sauce:

- Olive oil: 1 tablespoon
- Onion, finely chopped: 1 small (about 1/2 cup)
- Garlic, chopped: 2 cloves
- Canned crushed tomatoes: 14 oz
- Fresh basil leaves, chopped: 1/4 cup
- Salt: 1/2 teaspoon
- Black pepper: 1/4 teaspoon

Instructions:

Step 1: Preheat the oven to 400°F (200°C).

Step 2: In a large mixing bowl, combine turkey mince, cooked quinoa, chopped onion, chopped garlic, parsley, egg, salt, and black pepper. Mix until well combined.

Step 3: Form the mixture into meatballs, about 1 inch in diameter.

Step 4: Heat 1 tablespoon of olive oil in a skillet over medium heat.

Step 5: Sear the meatballs on all sides, about 2-3 minutes per side.

Step 6: Remove the seared meatballs from the skillet and set aside.

Step 7: In the same skillet, heat another tablespoon of olive oil over medium heat.

Step 8: Add the chopped onion and garlic. Sauté for about 2-3 minutes until softened.

Step 9: Stir in the crushed tomatoes, basil leaves, salt, and black pepper.

Step 10: Simmer the sauce for 10 minutes, stirring occasionally.

Step 11: Place the seared meatballs into a baking dish.

Step 12: Pour the tomato-basil sauce over the meatballs.

Step 13: Bake in the preheated oven for 15 minutes, until the meatballs are cooked through.

Step 14: Remove the dish from the oven and let it rest for a few minutes.

Step 15: Garnish with additional basil leaves if desired.

Step 16: Serve the turkey-quinoa meatballs hot with the tomato-basil sauce.

These tender meatballs are packed with protein and flavor, complemented by a rich tomato-basil sauce. A satisfying, healthy dish perfect for supporting liver wellness.

Nutritional info (per serving): Cal 320 | Carb 20g | Fat 12g | Prot 30g | Fib 4g | Sugar 5g.

48. Baked Lemon-Herb Chicken

Preparation Time: 10 min. | Cooking Time: 25 min. | Servings: 4 | Difficulty: Easy.

Ingredients:

- Chicken breasts: 4 (about 1.3 lbs)

- Olive oil: 2 tablespoons
- Lemon juice: 2 tablespoons
- Garlic, chopped: 3 cloves
- Fresh thyme, chopped: 1 tablespoon
- Fresh rosemary, chopped: 1 tablespoon
- Salt: 1 teaspoon
- Black pepper: 1/2 teaspoon
- Lemon slices: 1 lemon (for garnish)

Instructions:

Step 1: Preheat the oven to 200°C (400°F).

Step 2: In a small bowl, whisk together the olive oil, lemon juice, chopped garlic, thyme, rosemary, salt, and black pepper.

Step 3: Place the chicken breasts in a baking dish and pour the marinade over them, ensuring they are evenly coated. Marinate for at least 10 minutes or up to 30 minutes.

Step 4: Place lemon slices on each chicken breast for added flavor and garnish.

Step 5: Bake in the preheated oven for 20-25 minutes, until the chicken is fully cooked and no longer pink in the center.

Step 6: Remove the baked chicken from the oven and let it rest for a few minutes before serving.

Step 7: Serve hot, garnished with additional fresh herbs if desired.

This tender and flavorful chicken dish highlights the brightness of lemon and the aroma of fresh herbs. Perfect for a nutritious, liver-friendly meal.

Nutritional info (per serving): Cal 250 | Carb 2g | Fat 10g | Prot 35g | Fib 0g | Sugar 0g.

49. Asian-Inspired Turkey Salad Wraps

Preparation Time: 15 min. | Cooking Time: 15 min. | Servings: 4 | Difficulty: Easy.

Ingredients:

- Ground turkey: 1 lb
- Butter lettuce leaves: 1 head
- Olive oil: 2 tablespoons
- Garlic, chopped: 3 cloves
- Ginger, chopped: 1 tablespoon
- Low-sodium soy sauce: 3 tablespoons
- Hoisin sauce: 2 tablespoons
- Rice vinegar: 1 tablespoon
- Sriracha sauce: 1 tablespoon (adjust to taste)
- Green onions, thinly sliced: 2
- Carrot, julienned: 1 medium
- Water chestnuts, drained and chopped: 1 can (8 oz)
- Sesame oil: 1 teaspoon
- Salt: 1/2 teaspoon
- Black pepper: 1/4 teaspoon
- Sesame seeds: for garnish

Instructions:

Step 1: Carefully separate the leaves of the butter lettuce to form cups for the filling. Wash and pat dry the lettuce leaves, then set aside.

Step 2: Heat olive oil in a large pan over medium heat. Add chopped garlic and ginger and sauté for about 1 minute until fragrant.

Step 3: Add the ground turkey to the pan and cook until browned, breaking it apart with a spatula.

Step 4: In a small bowl, whisk together soy sauce, hoisin sauce, rice vinegar, and sriracha sauce.

Step 5: Once the turkey is fully cooked, add the green onions, julienned carrot, chopped water chestnuts, sesame oil, salt, and black pepper to the pan. Stir well until everything is well combined.

Step 6: Pour the sauce over the turkey mixture and stir until evenly coated. Continue cooking for another 2-3 minutes to allow the flavors to blend.

Step 7: Spoon the turkey filling into the lettuce cups.

Step 8: Garnish with sesame seeds and additional green onions, if desired.

Step 9: Serve the Asian-inspired turkey salad wraps immediately, allowing everyone to assemble their own wraps at the table.

These wraps are light, flavorful, and packed with protein. A great option for a healthy, liver-supporting meal with an Asian twist.

Nutritional info (per serving): Cal 280 | Carb 10g | Fat 12g | Prot 30g | Fib 2g | Sugar 3g.

50. Pan-Fried Chicken and Vegetables

Preparation Time: 15 min. | Cooking Time: 15 min. | Servings: 4 | Difficulty: Easy.

Ingredients:

- Chicken breast, thinly sliced: 1 lb
- Bell peppers (red and green), sliced: 2 medium
- Broccoli, cut into florets: 1 medium head (about 4 cups)
- Carrot, julienned: 1 large
- Sugar snap peas, trimmed: 1 1/2 cups
- Garlic, chopped: 3 cloves
- Ginger, chopped: 1 tablespoon
- Low-sodium soy sauce: 3 tablespoons
- Rice vinegar: 2 tablespoons
- Honey: 1 tablespoon

- Sesame oil: 1 tablespoon
- Cornstarch: 1 tablespoon
- Olive oil: 2 tablespoons
- Salt: 1/2 teaspoon
- Black pepper: 1/4 teaspoon
- Cooked brown rice or quinoa: for serving

Instructions:

Step 1: In a small bowl, whisk together soy sauce, rice vinegar, honey, sesame oil, and cornstarch until well combined. Set aside.

Step 2: Heat olive oil in a large pan or wok over medium-high heat.

Step 3: Add chopped garlic and ginger and sauté for about 1 minute until fragrant.

Step 4: Add the thinly sliced chicken breast to the pan and season with salt and black pepper. Cook until the chicken is no longer pink and starts to brown, about 5-6 minutes.

Step 5: Add the sliced bell peppers, carrots, broccoli florets, and sugar snap peas to the pan with the chicken. Continue to stir-fry for another 3-4 minutes until the vegetables are tender yet still crisp.

Step 6: Pour the prepared sauce over the chicken and vegetables in the pan. Stir well to ensure everything is evenly coated.

Step 7: Cook for an additional 2-3 minutes until the sauce thickens and coats the chicken and vegetables.

Step 8: Serve the chicken and vegetable stir-fry hot with cooked brown rice or quinoa.

This vibrant stir-fry is a colorful medley of flavors and textures. Packed with lean protein and fresh vegetables, it's both satisfying and nutrient-dense, a perfect choice for those seeking a healthy, liver-supporting meal that's quick to prepare.

Nutritional info (per serving): Cal 280 | Carb 20g | Fat 8g | Prot 30g | Fib 4g | Sugar 6g.

51. Pan-Fried Lean Beef and Broccoli

Preparation Time: 15 min. | Cooking Time: 15 min. | Servings: 4 | Difficulty: Easy.

Ingredients:

- Lean beef (sirloin or flank steak), thinly sliced: 1.1 lbs
- Broccoli, cut into florets: 1 medium head (about 4 cups)
- Garlic, chopped: 3 cloves
- Ginger, chopped: 1 tablespoon
- Low-sodium soy sauce: 3 tablespoons
- Rice vinegar: 2 tablespoons
- Honey (optional, can be substituted with a sugar-free sweetener): 1 tablespoon
- Sesame oil: 1 tablespoon
- Cornstarch (optional, can be omitted): 1 tablespoon
- Olive oil: 2 tablespoons
- Salt and pepper: to taste
- Cooked brown rice for serving (optional, can be replaced with cauliflower rice for a lower carbohydrate option)

Instructions:

Step 1: In a small bowl, whisk together soy sauce, rice vinegar, honey, sesame oil, and cornstarch. Set the sauce aside.

Step 2: Heat olive oil in a large pan or wok over medium-high heat.

Step 3: Add garlic and ginger and let them sizzle for about 1 minute until fragrant.

Step 4: Add the beef and season with a pinch of salt and pepper. Stir-fry until browned, about 3-4 minutes. Remove the beef and set aside.

Step 5: In the same pan, add broccoli florets with a splash of water. Cover and steam for about 3 minutes until the broccoli is tender yet still crisp.

Step 6: Return the beef to the pan.

Step 7: Pour the prepared sauce over the beef and broccoli. Stir well to ensure everything is evenly coated.

Step 8: Cook for an additional 2-3 minutes until the sauce thickens.

Step 9: Serve hot, optionally with cooked brown rice or cauliflower rice.

This savory dish offers a flavorful balance of lean beef and crisp broccoli, enhanced by a tangy soy-based sauce. It's a wholesome and hearty choice for a quick, liver-friendly meal packed with protein and nutrients.

Nutritional info (per serving): Cal 320 | Carb 25g | Fat 10g | Prot 30g | Fib 4g | Sugar 6g.

52. Spiced Beef Kabobs with Yogurt Sauce

Preparation Time: 20 min. | Cooking Time: 10 min. | Servings: 4 | Difficulty: Easy.

Ingredients:

- Lean beef (sirloin or tenderloin), cut into 1-inch cubes: 1.3 lbs
- Red bell pepper, diced: 1 large
- Yellow bell pepper, diced: 1 large
- Red onion, diced: 1 large
- Cherry tomatoes: 12-16
- Olive oil: 2 tablespoons
- Garlic, chopped: 3 cloves
- Ground cumin: 1 teaspoon
- Paprika: 1 teaspoon

Ground coriander: 1/2 teaspoon

- Salt: 1 teaspoon

- Black pepper: 1/2 teaspoon

For the Yogurt Sauce:

- Greek yogurt: 1 cup

- Lemon juice: 2 tablespoons

- Garlic, chopped: 1 clove

- Fresh parsley, chopped: 2 tablespoons

- Salt: 1/2 teaspoon

- Black pepper: 1/4 teaspoon

Instructions:

Step 1: In a bowl, mix together the olive oil, chopped garlic, ground cumin, paprika, ground coriander, salt, and black pepper.

Step 2: Add the beef cubes to the marinade and toss until evenly coated. Cover and refrigerate for at least 30 minutes or up to 2 hours.

Step 3: In another bowl, combine the Greek yogurt, lemon juice, chopped garlic, parsley, salt, and black pepper. Stir well until fully mixed. Keep refrigerated until serving.

Step 4: Preheat the grill or grill pan over medium-high heat.

Step 5: Thread the marinated beef cubes, bell peppers, red onion pieces, and cherry tomatoes onto skewers, alternating as desired.

Step 6: Place the assembled skewers on the preheated grill or grill pan.

Step 7: Grill for about 3-4 minutes on each side or until the beef is cooked to your desired doneness and the vegetables are tender and slightly charred.

Step 8: Serve the Spiced Beef Kabobs hot off the grill with the yogurt sauce for dipping.

This dish brings together tender beef and vibrant vegetables in a deliciously spiced marinade. Paired with a creamy yogurt sauce, it's a flavorful, protein-rich meal perfect for a health-conscious diet.

Nutritional info (per serving): Cal 320 | Carb 10g | Fat 12g | Prot 40g | Fib 2g | Sugar 4g.

53. Beef and Sweet Potato Stew

Preparation Time: 15 min. | Cooking Time: 90 min. | Servings: 4 | Difficulty: Medium.

Ingredients:

- Beef stew meat, cubed: 1.3 lbs

- Sweet potatoes, peeled and cubed: 2 medium (about 4 cups)

- Carrots, sliced: 2 medium (about 1 1/2 cups)

- Onion, chopped: 1 large (about 1 cup)

- Garlic, chopped: 3 cloves

- Tomato paste: 2 tablespoons

- Beef broth: 4 cups

- Worcestershire sauce: 2 tablespoons

- Thyme, dried: 1 teaspoon

- Rosemary, dried: 1 teaspoon

- Salt: 1 teaspoon

- Black pepper: 1/2 teaspoon

- Olive oil: 2 tablespoons

- Cornstarch (optional, for thickening): 2 tablespoons

- Water (optional, for thickening): 2 tablespoons

Instructions:

Step 1: Heat olive oil in a large pot or Dutch oven over medium-high heat.

Step 2: Add beef cubes and sear until browned on all sides, about 5-7 minutes. Remove the beef from the pot and set aside.

Step 3: In the same pot, add chopped onion and garlic. Sauté for about 2-3 minutes until fragrant.

Step 4: Return the seared beef to the pot.

Step 5: Add cubed sweet potatoes, sliced carrots, tomato paste, thyme, rosemary, salt, and black pepper. Stir to combine.

Step 6: Pour in the beef broth and Worcestershire sauce. Stir well.

Step 7: Bring the stew to a boil, then reduce heat to low. Cover and simmer for about 1 hour until the beef and vegetables are tender.

Step 8: If desired, mix cornstarch with water to form a slurry. Stir the slurry into the stew during the last 10 minutes of cooking to thicken the broth.

Step 9: Once the stew is cooked and thickened as desired, remove from heat.

Step 10: Serve the beef and sweet potato stew hot, garnished with fresh parsley if desired.

This hearty stew combines tender beef and sweet potatoes in a rich, savory broth. Perfect for a comforting meal, it's packed with protein and flavor.

Nutritional info (per serving): Cal 380 | Carb 35g | Fat 12g | Prot 30g | Fib 5g | Sugar 6g.

54. Beef with Balsamic Glaze and Roasted Vegetable Salad

Preparation Time: 15 min. | Cooking Time: 25 mins.| Servings: 4 | Difficulty: Medium.

Ingredients:
- Beef tenderloin steaks, thinly sliced: 1.1 lbs
- Bell peppers (red and yellow), sliced: 2
- Zucchini, sliced: 1 large
- Red onion, sliced: 1 large
- Cherry tomatoes: 1 cup
- Baby spinach: 4 cups
- Balsamic vinegar: 3 tablespoons
- Olive oil: 3 tablespoons
- Garlic, chopped: 2 cloves
- Dijon mustard: 1 tablespoon
- Honey: 1 tablespoon
- Salt: 1 teaspoon
- Black pepper: 1/2 teaspoon
- Fresh parsley: for garnish

Instructions:

Step 1: In a bowl, combine thinly sliced beef with chopped garlic, 2 tablespoons of balsamic vinegar, Dijon mustard, honey, salt, and black pepper. Marinate for at least 15 minutes.

Step 2: Preheat the oven to 200°C (400°F).

Step 3: Arrange sliced bell peppers, zucchini, red onions, and cherry tomatoes on a baking sheet.

Step 4: Drizzle with 1 tablespoon of olive oil and season with salt and black pepper. Toss to coat.

Step 5: Roast in the preheated oven for 20-25 minutes until vegetables are soft and slightly caramelized.

Step 6: Heat a pan over medium-high heat. Add marinated beef slices (discard excess marinade) and cook for 3-4 minutes per side or until desired doneness.

Step 7: In a small bowl, whisk together the remaining 1 tablespoon of balsamic vinegar and 2 tablespoons of olive oil. Season with salt and black pepper to taste.

Step 8: In a large bowl, combine the roasted vegetables, cooked beef slices, and baby spinach.

Step 9: Drizzle the salad with balsamic dressing and gently toss to combine.

Step 10: Plate the salad and garnish with fresh parsley.!

This flavorful salad balances tender beef, roasted vegetables, and a tangy balsamic glaze. A wholesome dish that's both nourishing and satisfying.

Nutritional info (per serving): Cal 380 | Carb 18g | Fat 22g | Prot 30g | Fib 5g | Sugar 10g.

55. Stuffed Bell Peppers with Ground Beef and Quinoa

Preparation Time: 20 min. | Cooking Time: 45 min. | Servings: 4 | Difficulty: Medium.

Ingredients:

- Bell peppers (red, yellow, or green): 4 large
- Lean ground beef: 1 lb
- Quinoa, cooked: 1 cup
- Onion, finely chopped: 1 medium (about 1 cup)
- Garlic, chopped: 3 cloves
- Tomato sauce: 1 cup
- Italian seasoning: 1 teaspoon
- Salt: 1 teaspoon
- Black pepper: 1/2 teaspoon
- Olive oil: 2 tablespoons
- Grated cheese (optional): for sprinkling
- Fresh parsley: for garnish

Instructions:

Step 1: Preheat the oven to 180°C (350°F).

Step 2: Cut the tops off the bell peppers and remove the seeds and membranes. Rinse the bell peppers under cold water.

Step 3: Cook the quinoa according to package instructions until soft and fluffy.

Step 4: Heat olive oil in a large pan over medium heat. Add chopped onion and garlic. Sauté for about 3-4 minutes until soft and fragrant.

Step 5: Add the ground beef to the pan. Break it up with a spoon and cook until browned and no longer pink, about 5-7 minutes.

Step 6: Stir in the cooked quinoa, tomato sauce, Italian seasoning, salt, and black pepper. Cook for another 2-3 minutes until the meat is done.

Step 7: Place the hollowed-out bell peppers in a baking dish. Evenly distribute the beef and quinoa mixture into each pepper.

Step 8: Cover the baking dish with aluminum foil and bake in the preheated oven for 25-30 minutes until the bell peppers are tender.

Step 9: If desired, sprinkle grated cheese over the stuffed bell peppers in the last 5 minutes of baking until melted and bubbly.

Step 10: Garnish the stuffed bell peppers with fresh parsley before serving.

This hearty dish combines the nutritional benefits of lean protein, fiber-rich quinoa, and vibrant bell peppers, offering a delicious and satisfying meal perfect for a fatty liver-friendly diet.

Nutritional info (per serving): Cal 380 | Carb 35g | Fat 15g | Prot 25g | Fib 7g | Sugar 8g.

56. Pork Tenderloin with Apple Cider Vinegar

Preparation Time: 10 min. | Cooking Time: 25 min. | Servings: 4 | Difficulty: Easy.

Ingredients:

- Pork tenderloin: 1.3 lbs
- Apple cider vinegar: 1/4 cup
- Olive oil: 2 tablespoons
- Garlic powder: 1 teaspoon
- Onion powder: 1 teaspoon

- Paprika: 1 teaspoon
- Salt: 1/2 teaspoon
- Black pepper: 1/2 teaspoon
- Fresh thyme (optional): for garnish

Instructions:

Step 1: Preheat your oven to 200°C (400°F).

Step 2: Trim any excess fat off the pork tenderloin and pat it dry with paper towels.

Step 3: In a small bowl, mix together the apple cider vinegar, olive oil, garlic powder, onion powder, paprika, salt, and black pepper to create a marinade.

Step 4: Rub the pork tenderloin with the marinade, ensuring it's evenly coated.

Step 5: Heat a large oven-proof skillet over medium-high heat. Once hot, add the pork tenderloin to the skillet and sear it for 2-3 minutes on each side until browned.

Step 6: Transfer the skillet to the preheated oven and roast the pork tenderloin for 15-20 minutes or until it reaches an internal temperature of 63°C (145°F).

Step 7: Remove the pork tenderloin from the oven and let it rest for 5 minutes before slicing.

Step 8: Cut the pork tenderloin into medallions and serve hot, garnished with fresh thyme if desired.

The tangy apple cider vinegar perfectly complements the tender pork, creating a flavorful dish that's both satisfying and light. Ideal for supporting a balanced and liver-friendly diet.

Nutritional info (per serving): Cal 280 | Carb 2g | Fat 12g | Prot 38g | Fib 0g | Sugar 1g.

57. Spiralized Zoodles with Spicy Pork and Vegetables

Preparation Time: 15 min. | Cooking Time: 15 min. | Servings: 4 | Difficulty: Easy.

Ingredients:

- Pork loin, thinly sliced: 1.1 lbs
- Zucchini: 4 medium (about 4 cups, sliced)
- Carrot: 2 large (about 2 cups, julienned)
- Bell pepper (any color), sliced: 1 large
- Onion, sliced: 1 large (about 1 cup)
- Garlic, minced: 3 cloves
- Low-sodium soy sauce: 3 tablespoons
- Rice vinegar: 2 tablespoons
- Sriracha sauce: 2 tablespoons
- Sesame oil: 1 tablespoon
- Olive oil: 2 tablespoons
- Salt: to taste
- Black pepper: to taste
- Sesame seeds, for garnishing: 1 tablespoon
- Green onions, chopped, for garnishing: 2 stalks

Instructions:

Step 1: Wash and peel the zucchinis and carrots.

Step 2: Use a spiralizer to create zucchini noodles and slice the carrots into thin strips.

Step 3: Slice the bell pepper and onion into thin slices.

Step 4: In a bowl, mix soy sauce, rice vinegar, Sriracha, garlic, sesame oil, salt, and black pepper.

Step 5: Add the pork slices to the marinade and let them sit for 10 minutes.

Step 6: Heat olive oil in a large skillet over medium-high heat.

Step 7: Add the bell peppers and onions and sauté for 3-4 minutes until slightly softened.

Step 8: Stir in the carrot strips and cook for 2 more minutes.

Step 9: Push the vegetables to one side of the skillet.

Step 10: Add the marinated pork slices and cook for 3-4 minutes until browned and fully cooked.

Step 11: Add the spiralized zucchini to the skillet and toss everything together.

Step 12: Cook for 2-3 minutes until the zucchini is tender yet crisp.

Step 13: Garnish with sesame seeds and chopped green onions before serving.

The combination of tender pork and vibrant vegetables makes this dish both flavorful and quick, perfectly suited to a liver-friendly diet.

Nutritional info (per serving): Cal 320 | Carb 14g | Fat 15g | Prot 32g | Fib 3g | Sugar 5g.

58. Pork and Pineapple Skewers

Preparation Time: 20 min. | Cooking Time: 10 min. | Servings: 4 | Difficulty: Easy.

Ingredients:

- Pork tenderloin, cubed: 1.1 lbs
- Pineapple, cubed: 1 small
- Red bell pepper, cubed: 1 large
- Red onion, cubed: 1 large
- Olive oil: 2 tablespoons
- Low-sodium soy sauce: 3 tablespoons
- Honey: 2 tablespoons
- Garlic, minced: 3 cloves
- Ground ginger: 1 teaspoon
- Salt: to taste
- Black pepper: to taste
- Wooden skewers, soaked in water: 8-10

Instructions:

Step 1: In a bowl, mix olive oil, soy sauce, honey, minced garlic, ground ginger, salt, and black pepper.

Step 2: Place the cubed pork tenderloin in a shallow dish or resealable plastic bag.

Step 3: Pour the marinade over the pork, ensuring it's evenly coated. Cover or seal and refrigerate for at least 30 minutes or up to 4 hours.

Step 4: Preheat the grill or grill pan to medium-high heat.

Step 5: Thread the marinated pork cubes, pineapple pieces, red bell pepper, and red onion alternately onto the soaked wooden skewers.

Step 6: Lightly oil the grill grates to prevent sticking.

Step 7: Place the skewers on the preheated grill and cook for 3-4 minutes on each side until the pork is cooked through and the vegetables are tender and slightly charred.

Step 8: Remove the skewers from the grill and let them rest for a few minutes.

Step 9: Serve hot, garnished with chopped fresh herbs if desired.

The smoky grill flavors pair wonderfully with the sweet pineapple, making this dish a tasty and wholesome option for a liver-friendly diet.

Nutritional info (per serving): Cal 320 | Carb 20g | Fat 12g | Prot 30g | Fib 2g | Sugar 10g.

59. Lean Pork Chop with Cauliflower Mash

Preparation Time: 15 mins | Cooking Time: 30 mins | Servings: 4 | Difficulty: Easy

Ingredients:

- Lean pork chops: 4 (each approx. 5.3 oz)
- Cauliflower, cut into florets: 1 large head (about 4-5 cups)
- Olive oil: 2 tablespoons
- Garlic, minced: 2 cloves
- Low-fat milk: 1/4 cup

- Reduced-sodium chicken broth: 1/4 cup

- Salt: to taste

- Black pepper: to taste

- Fresh parsley, chopped (for garnishing): optional

Instructions:

Season both sides of the pork chops with salt and pepper.

Heat 1 tablespoon of olive oil in a large skillet over medium-high heat.

Add the pork chops to the pan and cook for 3-4 minutes on each side until browned and cooked through. Remove from the pan and set aside.

In a large pot, bring water to a boil and add the cauliflower florets. Cook for about 10 minutes until the cauliflower is fork-tender.

Drain the cauliflower and return it to the pot.

In the same skillet used for the pork chops, heat the remaining tablespoon of olive oil over medium heat. Add the minced garlic and cook for 1-2 minutes until fragrant.

Add the cooked garlic to the pot with the cauliflower. Mash the cauliflower with a potato masher or immersion blender until smooth.

Gradually add the low-fat milk and reduced-sodium chicken broth to the cauliflower mash, stirring until creamy. Season with salt and pepper to taste.

Spread the cauliflower mash on serving plates and top each with a cooked pork chop.

Garnish with chopped fresh parsley if desired.

Nutritional Information (per serving): Calories 250| Fat 10g| Carbohydrates 8g| Protein 30g

60. Pork Tenderloin in Herb Crust with Roasted Root Vegetables

Preparation Time: 15 min. | Cooking Time: 30 min. | Servings: 4 | Difficulty: Easy.

Ingredients:

- Pork tenderloin, boneless: 1.3 lbs

- Potatoes, peeled and cubed: 1 lb

- Carrots, peeled and sliced: 10.5 oz

- Parsnips, peeled and sliced: 7 oz

- Olive oil: 3 tablespoons

- Dijon mustard: 2 tablespoons

- Garlic, minced: 2 cloves

- Fresh rosemary, chopped: 1 tablespoon

- Fresh thyme leaves: 1 tablespoon

- Salt: to taste

- Black pepper: to preference

Instructions:

Step 1: Season both sides of the pork chops with salt and pepper.

Step 2: Heat 1 tablespoon of olive oil in a large skillet over medium-high heat.

Step 3: Add the pork chops to the pan and cook for 3-4 minutes on each side until browned and cooked through. Remove from the pan and set aside.

Step 4: In a large pot, bring water to a boil and add the cauliflower florets.

Step 5: Cook the cauliflower for about 10 minutes until fork-tender, then drain and return to the pot.

Step 6: In the same skillet used for the pork chops, heat the remaining tablespoon of olive oil over medium heat.

Step 7: Add minced garlic and cook for 1-2 minutes until fragrant.

Step 8: Add the cooked garlic to the pot with the cauliflower.

Step 9: Mash the cauliflower with a potato masher or immersion blender until smooth.

Step 10: Gradually add low-fat milk and reduced-sodium chicken broth to the cauliflower mash, stirring until creamy.

Step 11: Season the mash with salt and pepper to taste.

Step 12: Spread the cauliflower mash on serving plates and top with a pork chop.

Step 13: Garnish with chopped fresh parsley if desired.

The creamy cauliflower mash pairs wonderfully with the lean pork chop, offering a satisfying meal that's both light and nutritious. Ideal for supporting liver health and a balanced diet.

Nutritional info (per serving): Cal 250 | Carb 8g | Fat 10g | Prot 30g | Fib 3g | Sugar 2g.

Chapter 6: Fish Dishes

Fresh and Heart-Healthy Recipes to Support Wellness

———— ❖ ————

61. Grilled Salmon with Avocado Salsa

Preparation Time: 15 mins | Cooking Time: 10 mins | Servings: 4 | Difficulty: Easy

Ingredients:

- Salmon fillets: 4 (each about 5.3 oz)
- Olive oil: 2 tablespoons
- Salt: 1 teaspoon
- Black pepper: 1/2 teaspoon

For the Avocado Salsa:

- Avocado, diced: 2
- Tomato, diced: 1 medium
- Red onion, finely chopped: 1/4 cup
- Fresh cilantro, chopped: 1/4 cup
- Lime juice: 2 tablespoons
- Garlic, minced: 1 clove
- Salt: 1/2 teaspoon
- Black pepper: 1/4 teaspoon

Instructions:

Step 1: Preheat the grill to medium-high heat.

Step 2: Pat the salmon fillets dry with paper towels and brush both sides with olive oil.

Step 3: Season the salmon fillets with salt and black pepper.

Step 4: Place the salmon fillets skin-side down on the preheated grill.

Step 5: Grill for about 4-5 minutes on each side or until the salmon is cooked through and flakes easily with a fork.

Step 6: In a medium bowl, mix the diced avocado, diced tomato, finely chopped red onion, chopped cilantro, lime juice, minced garlic, salt, and black pepper. Stir well.

Step 7: Remove the grilled salmon from the grill and place on serving plates.

Step 8: Top each salmon fillet with a generous spoonful of avocado salsa.

Step 9: Serve immediately, garnished with additional cilantro or lime wedges, if desired.

Nutritional Information (per serving): Calories 350| Fat 20g| Carbohydrates 8g| Protein 30g

62. Baked Cod with Lemon and Dill

Preparation Time: 15 min. | Cooking Time: 10 min. | Servings: 4 | Difficulty: Easy.

Ingredients:

Cod fillets: 4 (each about 5.3 oz)

Lemon, thinly sliced: 1

- Fresh dill, chopped: 2 tablespoons
- Olive oil: 2 tablespoons
- Salt: 1 teaspoon
- Black pepper: 1/2 teaspoon
- Garlic powder: 1/2 teaspoon
- Paprika: 1/2 teaspoon
- Lemon wedges: for serving

Instructions:

Step 1: Preheat the oven to 200°C (400°F) and line a baking sheet with parchment paper.

Step 2: Pat the cod fillets dry with paper towels and place them on the prepared baking sheet.

Step 3: Drizzle the fillets with olive oil and season with salt, black pepper, garlic powder, and paprika.

Step 4: Top each fillet with a few slices of lemon and sprinkle with fresh dill.

Step 5: Bake the cod in the preheated oven for 10-12 minutes, or until the fish is opaque and flakes easily with a fork.

Step 6: Remove from the oven and let rest for a minute.

Step 7: Serve the baked cod hot with lemon wedges on the side.

This vibrant dish combines the smoky flavors of grilled salmon with the freshness of avocado salsa, creating a meal that is both delicious and liver-friendly.

Nutritional info (per serving): Cal 350 | Carb 8g | Fat 20g | Prot 30g | Fib 4g | Sugar 2g.

63. TUNA AND CHICKPEA SALAD

Preparation Time: 10 min. | Cooking Time: 0 min. | Servings: 4 | Difficulty: Easy.

Ingredients:

- Canned tuna in water, drained: 2 cans
- Chickpeas, drained and rinsed: 1 can
- Cherry tomatoes, halved: 1 cup
- Cucumber, diced: 1 medium
- Red onion, thinly sliced: 1/2 medium
- Kalamata olives, pitted and halved: 1/4 cup
- Fresh parsley, chopped: 1/4 cup
- Extra virgin olive oil: 2 tablespoons
- Lemon juice: 2 tablespoons
- Salt: 1/2 teaspoon
- Black pepper: 1/4 teaspoon
- Mixed salad greens: 4 cups

Instructions:

Step 1: In a small bowl, whisk together olive oil, lemon juice, salt, and black pepper to make the dressing.

Step 2: In a large bowl, combine drained tuna, chickpeas, halved cherry tomatoes, diced cucumber, sliced red onion, halved Kalamata olives, and chopped fresh parsley.

Step 3: Pour the dressing over the tuna and chickpea mixture and gently toss to coat evenly.

Step 4: Distribute the mixed salad greens evenly among four plates.

Step 5: Top each plate with the tuna and chickpea mixture.

Step 6: Serve immediately.

The combination of fresh vegetables and protein-rich tuna makes this salad a satisfying, quick meal that's both delicious and nourishing for liver health.

Nutritional info (per serving): Cal 280 | Carb 20g | Fat 12g | Prot 22g | Fib 5g | Sugar 3g.

64. Steamed Trout in Asian Style

Preparation Time: 15 min. | Cooking Time: 15 min. | Servings: 2 | Difficulty: Easy.

Ingredients:

- Trout fillets: 2

- Soy sauce: 2 tablespoons

- Rice vinegar: 1 tablespoon

- Fresh ginger, grated: 1 tablespoon

- Garlic cloves, chopped: 2

- Sesame oil: 1 teaspoon

- Green onions, thinly sliced: 2

- Sesame seeds: 1 tablespoon, for garnish

- Steamed rice or vegetables: for serving

Instructions:

Step 1: Fill a steamer insert with water and bring it to a boil. Place a steaming basket or rack in the pot.

Step 2: Season both sides of the trout fillets with salt and pepper.

Step 3: In a small bowl, mix soy sauce, rice vinegar, grated ginger, chopped garlic, and sesame oil to make a sauce.

Step 4: Place the seasoned trout fillets in the steaming basket, ensuring they do not overlap.

Step 5: Pour half of the sauce over the trout fillets, reserving the rest for serving.

Step 6: Cover the steamer and steam the trout for about 8-10 minutes, until cooked through and flaky.

Step 7: Carefully transfer the steamed trout fillets to serving plates.

Step 8: Drizzle the remaining sauce over the trout fillets.

Step 9: Garnish with sliced green onions and sesame seeds.

Step 10: Serve immediately with steamed rice or vegetables.

The delicate flavors of this dish highlight the natural freshness of trout, making it a satisfying and wholesome choice. Quick to prepare and packed with nutrients, it's perfect for a liver-friendly diet.

Nutritional info (per serving): Cal 250 | Carb 5g | Fat 12g | Prot 30g | Fib 0g | Sugar 1g.

65. Spicy Shrimp and Quinoa Bowl

Preparation Time: 15 min. | Cooking Time: 20 min. | Servings: 2 | Difficulty: Easy.

Ingredients:

- Shrimp, peeled and deveined: 1/2 pound

- Quinoa, uncooked: 1 cup

- Olive oil: 2 tablespoons

- Garlic, chopped: 2 cloves

- Red chili flakes: 1 teaspoon (adjust to taste)

- Paprika: 1 teaspoon

- Salt: 1/2 teaspoon

- Black pepper: 1/4 teaspoon

- Cherry tomatoes, halved: 1 cup

- Spinach leaves: 2 cups

- Lemon, juiced: 1

- Fresh parsley, chopped: 2 tablespoons

- Avocado, sliced (optional, for serving): 1

Instructions:

Step 1: Rinse the quinoa under cold water.

Step 2: In a medium pot, combine the quinoa with 2 cups of water. Bring to a boil, then reduce the heat and simmer covered for about 15 minutes until cooked. Remove from heat and fluff with a fork.

Step 3: In a bowl, toss the shrimp with chopped garlic, red chili flakes, paprika, salt, and black pepper.

Step 4: Heat 1 tablespoon of olive oil in a large pan over medium-high heat.

Step 5: Add the seasoned shrimp to the pan and cook for 2-3 minutes on each side until pink and opaque. Remove from the pan and set aside.

Step 6: In the same pan, heat the remaining tablespoon of olive oil.

Step 7: Add the halved cherry tomatoes and cook for 2-3 minutes until they start to soften.

Step 8: Add the cooked quinoa and spinach leaves to the pan. Stir until the spinach wilts and everything is heated through.

Step 9: Remove from heat, squeeze the lemon juice over the quinoa mixture, and toss with chopped parsley.

Step 10: Divide the quinoa mixture evenly between two bowls and top with the cooked spicy shrimp.

Step 11: Optionally garnish with avocado slices before serving.

This vibrant dish combines the bold flavors of spicy shrimp with wholesome quinoa, creating a balanced, satisfying meal. Packed with nutrients, it's ideal for a healthy lifestyle.

Nutritional info (per serving): Cal 450 | Carb 45g | Fat 15g | Prot 30g | Fib 8g | Sugar 5g.

66. Baked Mediterranean Mackerel

Preparation Time: 15 min. | Cooking Time: 20 min. | Servings: 2 | Difficulty: Easy.

Ingredients:
- Mackerel fillets: 2 fillets
- Olive oil: 2 tablespoons
- Garlic, chopped: 2 cloves
- Cherry tomatoes, halved: 1 cup
- Kalamata olives, pitted and halved: 1/4 cup
- Capers: 2 tablespoons
- Fresh parsley, chopped: 2 tablespoons
- Lemon, thinly sliced: 1
- Salt: 1/2 teaspoon
- Black pepper: 1/4 teaspoon
- Dried oregano: 1 teaspoon
- Lemon zest: 1 teaspoon

Instructions:
Step 1: Preheat the oven to 200°C (400°F).

Step 2: Pat the mackerel fillets dry with paper towels and place them on a baking sheet lined with parchment paper.

Step 3: Drizzle the fillets with 1 tablespoon of olive oil and sprinkle with chopped garlic, salt, and black pepper.

Step 4: In a bowl, mix cherry tomatoes, Kalamata olives, capers, parsley, lemon slices, and lemon zest.

Step 5: Drizzle the mixture with the remaining tablespoon of olive oil, season with oregano, salt, and pepper, and toss well.

Step 6: Spread the Mediterranean topping evenly over the mackerel fillets.

Step 7: Place the baking sheet in the oven and bake for 15-20 minutes, until the mackerel is cooked through and flakes easily with a fork.

Step 8: Remove the mackerel from the oven and let it rest for a few minutes before serving.

Step 9: Serve the baked mackerel hot, garnished with fresh parsley if desired.

The rich Mediterranean flavors perfectly complement the tender mackerel, offering a nourishing dish full of vibrant and fresh ingredients. It's an excellent choice for a healthy, liver-friendly meal.

Nutritional info (per serving): Cal 350 | Carb 5g | Fat 20g | Prot 30g | Fib 2g | Sugar 1g.

67. Spicy Lime and Cilantro Tilapia

Preparation Time: 10 min. | Cooking Time: 15 min. | Servings: 2 | Difficulty: Easy.

Ingredients:

- Tilapia fillets: 2 fillets
- Lime juice: 2 tablespoons
- Lime zest: 1 teaspoon
- Fresh cilantro, chopped: 2 tablespoons
- Garlic, chopped: 2 cloves
- Olive oil: 2 tablespoons
- Salt: 1/2 teaspoon
- Black pepper: 1/4 teaspoon
- Paprika: 1/2 teaspoon
- Cayenne pepper (optional): 1/4 teaspoon

Instructions:

Step 1: In a shallow dish, mix lime juice, lime zest, chopped cilantro, garlic, olive oil, salt, black pepper, paprika, and cayenne pepper (if using).

Step 2: Place the tilapia fillets in the marinade, turning them to coat evenly. Let them marinate for at least 10 minutes.

Step 3: Heat a non-stick skillet over medium heat and lightly grease with olive oil or cooking spray.

Step 4: Add the marinated tilapia fillets to the hot skillet, shaking off any excess marinade.

Step 5: Cook the tilapia for 3-4 minutes on each side, until golden brown and cooked through. The fish should flake easily with a fork when done.

Step 6: Remove the tilapia from the skillet and place on serving plates.

Step 7: Garnish with additional chopped cilantro and a lime wedge, if desired.

Step 8: Serve the spicy lime and cilantro tilapia hot, accompanied by your favorite sides.

This zesty dish combines bold flavors with a light texture, creating a perfectly balanced meal. Its quick preparation makes it a great choice for a healthy weeknight dinner.

Nutritional info (per serving): Cal 200 | Carb 2g | Fat 10g | Prot 25g | Fib 0g | Sugar 0g.

68. Salmon and Spinach Quiche

Preparation Time: 15 min. | Cooking Time: 40 min. | Servings: 4 | Difficulty: Medium.

Ingredients:

- Frozen pie crust: 1 (store-bought or homemade)
- Salmon fillet, cooked and flaked: 1 fillet
- Spinach, fresh or frozen, chopped: 1 1/2 cups
- Eggs: 4 large
- Milk: 1 cup
- Cheddar cheese, grated: 1/2 cup
- Onion, finely chopped: 1 small
- Garlic, chopped: 2 cloves
- Olive oil: 1 tablespoon
- Salt: 1/2 teaspoon
- Black pepper: 1/4 teaspoon
- Nutmeg (optional): 1/4 teaspoon

Instructions:

Step 1: Preheat your oven to 180°C (350°F).

Step 2: If using a frozen pie crust, thaw it according to package instructions. For a homemade crust, pre-bake it for 10 minutes until lightly golden.

Step 3: Heat olive oil in a skillet over medium heat.

Step 4: Add chopped onion and garlic to the skillet and sauté until softened.

Step 5: Add chopped spinach to the skillet and cook until wilted. Remove excess moisture by pressing it between paper towels.

Step 6: Evenly distribute flaked salmon over the bottom of the pre-baked pie crust.

Step 7: Cover the salmon with the cooked spinach mixture.

Step 8: In a mixing bowl, whisk together eggs, milk, cheddar cheese, salt, pepper, and nutmeg (if using).

Step 9: Carefully pour the egg mixture over the salmon and spinach in the pie crust.

Step 10: Place the quiche in the preheated oven and bake for 30-35 minutes until the filling is set and golden brown.

Step 11: Remove from the oven and let cool for a few minutes before slicing.

Step 12: Serve warm or at room temperature.

This hearty quiche combines the richness of salmon with the freshness of spinach, offering a savory dish perfect for any occasion. It's satisfying and full of balanced nutrients.

Nutritional info (per serving): Cal 350 | Carb 20g | Fat 20g | Prot 25g | Fib 2g | Sugar 3g.

69. Halibut in Herb Crust with Roasted Vegetables

Preparation Time: 15 min. | Cooking Time: 25 min. | Servings: 2 | Difficulty: Easy.

Ingredients:
- Halibut: 2 fillets
- Olive oil: 2 tablespoons
- Garlic, chopped: 2 cloves
- Lemon zest: 1 teaspoon
- Fresh parsley, finely chopped: 2 tablespoons
- Fresh thyme, finely chopped: 1 tablespoon
- Salt: 1/2 teaspoon
- Black pepper: 1/4 teaspoon
- Mixed vegetables (e.g., bell peppers, zucchini, cherry tomatoes), diced: 3 cups
- Balsamic vinegar: 2 tablespoons

Instructions:
Step 1: Preheat the oven to 200°C (400°F).

Step 2: In a small bowl, mix olive oil, chopped garlic, lemon zest, parsley, thyme, salt, and black pepper to form a paste.

Step 3: Pat the halibut fillets dry with paper towels.

Step 4: Place the halibut fillets on a parchment paper-lined baking sheet.

Step 5: Spread the herb crust mixture evenly over each halibut fillet.

Step 6: In a separate bowl, toss the diced mixed vegetables with olive oil, salt, and black pepper.

Step 7: Spread the seasoned vegetables on another parchment paper-lined baking sheet.

Step 8: Place both baking sheets in the preheated oven.

Step 9: Bake the halibut for 12-15 minutes, until cooked through and flaky.

Step 10: Roast the vegetables for 20-25 minutes, until tender and caramelized.

Step 11: Remove the halibut and vegetables from the oven. Drizzle the roasted vegetables with balsamic vinegar.

Step 12: Serve the halibut with the roasted vegetables.

The aromatic herb crust elevates the halibut to a new level, while the roasted vegetables provide a delicious and nutrient-packed side. This is a balanced meal ideal for any healthy diet.

Nutritional info (per serving): Cal 350 | Carb 20g | Fat 15g | Prot 30g | Fib 6g | Sugar 7g.

70. Smoked Trout Salad with Mixed Greens

Preparation Time: 10 min. | Cooking Time: 0 min. | Servings: 2 | Difficulty: Easy.

Ingredients:

- Smoked trout fillets: 7 oz
- Mixed leafy greens: 5 oz
- Cherry tomatoes, halved: 1/2 cup
- Cucumber, thinly sliced: 1/2
- Red onion, thinly sliced: 1/4
- Avocado, sliced: 1
- Lemon, juiced: 1
- Olive oil: 2 tablespoons
- Dijon mustard: 1 teaspoon
- Honey: 1 teaspoon
- Salt: 1/4 teaspoon
- Black pepper: 1/4 teaspoon
- Fresh dill, chopped (optional, for garnish): 1 tablespoon

Instructions:

Step 1: In a small bowl, whisk together olive oil, Dijon mustard, honey, lemon juice, salt, and black pepper to make the dressing.

Step 2: In a large salad bowl, combine mixed greens, cherry tomatoes, cucumber slices, and red onion slices.

Step 3: Drizzle the dressing over the salad and gently toss to coat evenly.

Step 4: Break the smoked trout fillets into smaller pieces and scatter them over the salad.

Step 5: Divide the salad evenly between two plates.

Step 6: Top each serving with sliced avocado.

Step 7: Garnish with chopped fresh dill if desired.

Step 8: Serve immediately.

This vibrant salad offers a delightful combination of smoky trout, crisp vegetables, and creamy avocado. It's a light and nutritious option for a quick, healthy meal.

Nutritional info (per serving): Cal 280 | Carb 14g | Fat 18g | Prot 18g | Fib 5g | Sugar 6g.

71. Grilled Sardines with Pesto

Preparation Time: 10 min. | Cooking Time: 10 min. | Servings: 2 | Difficulty: Easy.

Ingredients:

- Fresh sardines: 14 oz (about 4 large sardines), cleaned and gutted
- Pesto sauce: 4 tablespoons
- Olive oil: 2 tablespoons
- Lemon, sliced: 1
- Salt: 1/2 teaspoon
- Black pepper: 1/4 teaspoon
- Fresh parsley, chopped (for garnish): 2 tablespoons

Instructions:

Step 1: Rinse the sardines under cold water and pat dry with paper towels.

Step 2: Make 2-3 diagonal cuts on each side of the sardines to ensure even cooking and flavor absorption.

Step 3: In a shallow dish, mix olive oil, salt, and black pepper.

Step 4: Add the sardines to the marinade, turning to coat evenly. Let them marinate for 10 minutes.

Step 5: Preheat a grill or grill pan over medium-high heat.

Step 6: Place the marinated sardines on the grill and cook for 3-4 minutes on each side until fully cooked and grill marks appear.

Step 7: Spread 1 tablespoon of pesto sauce over each sardine.

Step 8: Transfer the grilled sardines to a serving platter.

Step 9: Garnish with chopped parsley and lemon slices.

Step 10: Serve hot and enjoy.

The bold flavors of fresh pesto pair beautifully with the smoky sardines, creating a nutritious dish that's both satisfying and full of healthy fats.

Nutritional info (per serving): Cal 330 | Carb 2g | Fat 24g | Prot 27g | Fib 1g | Sugar 0g.

72. Honey-Glazed Salmon with Quinoa Pilaf

Preparation Time: 10 min. | Cooking Time: 20 min. | Servings: 2 | Difficulty: Easy.

Ingredients:

For the Honey-Glazed Salmon:
- Salmon fillets: 2
- Honey: 2 tablespoons
- Soy sauce: 1 tablespoon
- Olive oil: 1 tablespoon
- Lemon juice: 1 tablespoon
- Garlic, minced: 2 cloves
- Salt: 1/2 teaspoon
- Black pepper: 1/4 teaspoon

For the Quinoa Pilaf:
- Quinoa, rinsed: 1 cup
- Vegetable broth: 2 cups
- Olive oil: 1 tablespoon
- Onion, finely chopped: 1 small
- Carrot, diced: 1 medium
- Red bell pepper, diced: 1/2
- Frozen peas: 1/2 cup
- Garlic, minced: 2 cloves
- Salt: 1/2 teaspoon
- Black pepper: 1/4 teaspoon
- Fresh parsley, chopped (for garnish): 2 tablespoons

Instructions:

Step 1: In a small bowl, mix honey, soy sauce, olive oil, lemon juice, minced garlic, salt, and black pepper.

Step 2: Place the salmon fillets in a flat dish and pour the marinade over them, ensuring they are well coated. Let them marinate for 15 minutes.

Step 3: Heat olive oil in a pot over medium heat and sauté the chopped onion until translucent.

Step 4: Stir in the diced carrot, red bell pepper, frozen peas, minced garlic, salt, and black pepper. Cook for 2-3 minutes.

Step 5: Add the rinsed quinoa to the pot and mix well with the vegetables.

Step 6: Pour in the vegetable broth, bring to a boil, then reduce the heat to low. Cover and simmer for 15 minutes until the quinoa is cooked and liquid is absorbed. Fluff with a fork.

Step 7: Preheat the oven to 200°C (400°F) and line a baking sheet with parchment paper.

Step 8: Place the marinated salmon fillets on the prepared baking sheet.

Step 9: Bake for 12-15 minutes, until the salmon is fully cooked and flakes easily with a fork.

Step 10: Serve the quinoa pilaf on plates, topped with the honey-glazed salmon fillets.

Step 11: Garnish with chopped parsley and serve hot.

This dish combines tender honey-glazed salmon with a colorful quinoa pilaf, delivering a nutrient-rich and balanced meal. It's a perfect harmony of flavor and healthy ingredients.

Nutritional info (per serving): Cal 520 | Carb 45g | Fat 20g | Prot 38g | Fib 6g | Sugar 10g.

73. FISH TACOS WITH SLAW

Preparation Time: 15 min. | Cooking Time: 15 min. | Servings: 4 | Difficulty: Easy.

Ingredients:

For the Fish Tacos:

- White fish fillets (such as cod or tilapia): 1 lb
- Olive oil: 2 tablespoons
- Paprika: 1 teaspoon
- Cumin: 1 teaspoon
- Garlic powder: 1/2 teaspoon
- Salt: 1/2 teaspoon
- Black pepper: 1/4 teaspoon
- Corn tortillas: 8

For the Slaw:

- Red cabbage, thinly sliced: 2 cups
- Green cabbage, thinly sliced: 2 cups
- Carrot, grated: 1 large
- Fresh cilantro, chopped: 1/4 cup
- Lime juice: 2 tablespoons
- Olive oil: 1 tablespoon
- Honey: 1 tablespoon
- Salt: 1/2 teaspoon
- Black pepper: 1/4 teaspoon

To Serve:

- Avocado, sliced: 1
- Lime wedges
- Hot sauce (optional)

Instructions:

Step 1: Pat the fish fillets dry with paper towels and cut them into taco-sized pieces.

Step 2: In a small bowl, mix olive oil, paprika, cumin, garlic powder, salt, and black pepper to make a marinade.

Step 3: Coat the fish pieces evenly with the marinade.

Step 4: Heat a non-stick skillet over medium-high heat and add a bit of olive oil.

Step 5: Cook the fish for 3-4 minutes on each side until fully cooked and flaky. Remove from the skillet and set aside.

Step 6: In a large bowl, combine red cabbage, green cabbage, grated carrot, and chopped cilantro.

Step 7: In a small bowl, whisk together lime juice, olive oil, honey, salt, and black pepper to make the slaw dressing.

Step 8: Pour the dressing over the cabbage mixture and toss until well coated.

Step 9: Warm the corn tortillas in a pan or microwave.

Step 10: Place a portion of cooked fish on each tortilla.

Step 11: Top with slaw and avocado slices.

Step 12: Serve with lime wedges and hot sauce, if desired.

These fish tacos are packed with fresh, zesty flavors and complemented by a crunchy slaw, creating a light yet satisfying meal. Perfect for a healthy and quick dinner.

Nutritional info (per serving): Cal 350 | Carb 38g | Fat 12g | Prot 25g | Fib 7g | Sugar 6g.

74. SEA BASS WITH MEDITERRANEAN SALSA

Preparation Time: 15 min. | Cooking Time: 15 min. | Servings: 4 | Difficulty: Easy.

Ingredients:

For the Sea Bass:
- Sea bass fillets: 4
- Olive oil: 2 tablespoons
- Lemon juice: 2 tablespoons
- Garlic powder: 1 teaspoon
- Dried oregano: 1 teaspoon
- Salt: 1/2 teaspoon
- Black pepper: 1/4 teaspoon

For the Mediterranean Salsa:
- Cherry tomatoes, halved: 1 1/2 cups
- Cucumber, diced: 1/2
- Red onion, finely chopped: 1/2
- Kalamata olives, pitted and sliced: 1/4 cup
- Fresh parsley, chopped: 1/4 cup
- Feta cheese, crumbled: 1/4 cup
- Olive oil: 2 tablespoons
- Red wine vinegar: 1 tablespoon
- Salt: 1/2 teaspoon
- Black pepper: 1/4 teaspoon

Instructions:

Step 1: In a small bowl, mix olive oil, lemon juice, garlic powder, dried oregano, salt, and black pepper to create a marinade.

Step 2: Place the sea bass fillets in a shallow dish and pour the marinade over them, ensuring they are evenly coated. Marinate for about 10 minutes.

Step 3: Preheat the grill or grill pan to medium-high heat.

Step 4: Place the marinated sea bass fillets on the grill and cook for 4-5 minutes on each side until opaque and flaky.

Step 5: In a large bowl, combine halved cherry tomatoes, diced cucumber, finely chopped red onion, sliced Kalamata olives, chopped parsley, and crumbled feta cheese.

Step 6: Drizzle olive oil and red wine vinegar over the salsa. Season with salt and black pepper, then gently toss.

Step 7: Arrange the grilled sea bass fillets on serving plates.

Step 8: Top each fillet with a generous portion of Mediterranean salsa.

Step 9: Garnish with additional parsley, if desired.

Step 10: Serve immediately and enjoy!

The bright flavors of the Mediterranean salsa complement the tender sea bass beautifully, offering a fresh and nutrient-rich dish. A perfect choice for a light and balanced meal.

Nutritional info (per serving): Cal 280 | Carb 8g | Fat 14g | Prot 30g | Fib 2g | Sugar 3g.

75. Curry Shrimp and Cauliflower Rice

Preparation Time: 10 min. | Cooking Time: 20 min. | Servings: 4 | Difficulty: Easy.

Ingredients:

For the Curry Shrimp:
- Shrimps, peeled and deveined: 1 pound
- Olive oil: 2 tablespoons
- Onion, finely chopped: 1 large
- Garlic, chopped: 3 cloves
- Curry powder: 2 tablespoons
- Turmeric: 1 teaspoon
- Paprika: 1 teaspoon
- Cumin: 1 teaspoon
- Salt: 1/2 teaspoon
- Black pepper: 1/4 teaspoon
- Coconut milk: 1 cup
- Fresh coriander: for garnish

For the Cauliflower Rice:

- Cauliflower, cut into florets: 1 large head
- Olive oil: 1 tablespoon
- Salt: 1/2 teaspoon
- Black pepper: 1/4 teaspoon
- Fresh parsley: for garnish

Instructions:

Step 1: Pulse the cauliflower florets in a food processor until they resemble rice grains.

Step 2: Heat olive oil in a large skillet over medium heat.

Step 3: Add the cauliflower rice to the skillet and season with salt and black pepper.

Step 4: Cook for 5-7 minutes, stirring occasionally, until the cauliflower is soft. Set aside.

Step 5: In the same skillet, heat olive oil over medium heat.

Step 6: Add chopped onion and garlic to the skillet and sauté until soft.

Step 7: Stir in curry powder, turmeric, paprika, cumin, salt, and black pepper. Cook for 1-2 minutes until fragrant.

Step 8: Add the shrimps to the skillet and cook for 2-3 minutes on each side until pink and opaque.

Step 9: Pour in the coconut milk and stir well to combine. Let it simmer for 5 minutes until the sauce thickens slightly.

Step 10: Divide the cauliflower rice among serving plates.

Step 11: Top each plate with the curry shrimp mixture.

Step 12: Garnish with fresh coriander and parsley. Serve hot.

This flavorful dish combines aromatic curry spices with tender shrimp and light cauliflower rice, offering a satisfying and healthy meal.

Nutritional info (per serving): Cal 280 | Carb 10g | Fat 15g | Prot 25g | Fib 4g | Sugar 3g.

Chapter 7: Vegetarian Dishes

Plant-Based Options for Balanced Nutrition

———— ❖ ————

76. Quinoa and Black Bean Chili

Preparation Time: 15 min. | Cooking Time: 30 min. | Servings: 4 | Difficulty: Medium

Ingredients:

- Quinoa, rinsed: 1 cup
- Olive oil: 2 tablespoons
- Onion, chopped: 1 large
- Bell peppers (red and green), chopped: 1 each
- Garlic, chopped: 3 cloves
- Chili powder: 2 tablespoons
- Ground cumin: 1 tablespoon
- Paprika: 1 teaspoon
- Dried oregano: 1 teaspoon
- Crushed tomatoes: 1 can
- Black beans, drained and rinsed: 1 can
- Vegetable broth: 2 cups
- Salt: 1 teaspoon
- Black pepper: 1/2 teaspoon
- Fresh cilantro: for garnishing
- Lime wedges: for serving

Instructions:

Step 1: Rinse the quinoa under cold water.

Step 2: In a medium pot, combine the rinsed quinoa with 2 cups of water.

Step 3: Bring the pot to a boil, then reduce heat, cover, and simmer for 15 minutes until the quinoa is cooked and the water is absorbed.

Step 4: Set the cooked quinoa aside.

Step 5: Heat olive oil in a large pot over medium heat.

Step 6: Add the chopped onion and bell peppers to the pot and sauté for about 5 minutes until softened.

Step 7: Add garlic, chili powder, cumin, paprika, and oregano to the pot.

Step 8: Stir well and cook for 1-2 minutes until the spices are fragrant.

Step 9: Add the crushed tomatoes to the pot and stir to combine.

Step 10: Add the black beans and mix thoroughly.

Step 11: Stir in the cooked quinoa and vegetable broth, ensuring everything is evenly mixed.

Step 12: Season the mixture with salt and black pepper to taste.

Step 13: Bring the chili to a gentle simmer, then reduce the heat to low.

Step 14: Cover the pot and cook for 15-20 minutes, stirring occasionally to allow the flavors to meld.

Step 15: Taste the chili and adjust the seasoning if necessary.

Step 16: Ladle the chili into bowls for serving.

Step 17: Garnish each bowl with fresh cilantro and serve with lime wedges on the side for a burst of freshness.

This hearty chili blends the wholesome goodness of quinoa with the rich flavors of beans and spices, offering a comforting and nutritious meal. Perfect for a balanced and satisfying diet.

Nutritional info (per serving): Cal 350 | Carb 60g | Fat 6g | Prot 15g | Fib 8g | Sugar 6g.

77. Stuffed Portobello Mushrooms with Lentils and Spinach

Preparation Time: 15 min. | Cooking Time: 25 min. | Servings: 2 | Difficulty: Medium.

Ingredients:

- Portobello mushrooms: 4 large
- Olive oil: 2 tablespoons
- Garlic, finely chopped: 2 cloves
- Onion, finely chopped: 1 small
- Lentils, cooked: 1 cup
- Spinach, chopped: 2 cups
- Cherry tomatoes, halved: 1/2 cup
- Feta cheese, crumbled: 1/4 cup
- Salt: 1/2 teaspoon
- Black pepper: 1/4 teaspoon
- Italian seasoning: 1 teaspoon
- Parmesan cheese, grated (optional): 2 tablespoons
- Fresh parsley: for garnishing

Instructions:

Step 1: Preheat the oven to 190°C (375°F). Line a baking sheet with parchment paper.

Step 2: Remove the stems of the Portobello mushrooms and carefully scrape out the gills with a spoon.

Step 3: Place the mushrooms gill side up on the prepared baking sheet.

Step 4: Heat olive oil in a skillet over medium heat. Add chopped garlic and onion and sauté until soft.

Step 5: Add cooked lentils, chopped spinach, and halved cherry tomatoes to the skillet. Cook until the spinach wilts and the tomatoes soften, about 3-4 minutes.

Step 6: Season with salt, black pepper, and Italian seasoning. Stir well to combine.

Step 7: Evenly distribute the lentil-spinach mixture onto the Portobello mushrooms, pressing down slightly to compact the filling.

Step 8: Sprinkle the crumbled feta cheese over the stuffed mushrooms.

Step 9: Bake in the preheated oven for 20-25 minutes, until the mushrooms are tender and the filling is heated through.

Step 10: Remove the stuffed mushrooms from the oven and sprinkle with grated Parmesan cheese (if using) and fresh parsley.

Step 11: Serve hot and enjoy!

These stuffed Portobello mushrooms offer a flavorful and nutritious option, blending the earthiness of mushrooms with the hearty texture of lentils and fresh spinach.

Nutritional info (per serving): Cal 320 | Carb 40g | Fat 12g | Prot 15g | Fib 8g | Sugar 5g.

78. Sweet Potato and Kale Curry

Preparation Time: 15 min. | Cooking Time: 25 min. | Servings: 4 | Difficulty: Easy.

Ingredients:

- Sweet potatoes, peeled and cubed: 2 medium
- Kale, stems removed and leaves chopped: 4 cups

- Olive oil: 2 tablespoons
- Onion, chopped: 1 large
- Garlic, chopped: 3 cloves
- Ginger, grated: 1 tablespoon
- Curry powder: 2 tablespoons
- Ground turmeric: 1 teaspoon
- Cumin seeds: 1 teaspoon
- Coconut milk: 1 can (14 oz)
- Vegetable broth: 1 cup
- Salt: 1 teaspoon
- Black pepper: 1/2 teaspoon
- Fresh cilantro: for garnishing
- Cooked rice or naan bread: for serving

Instructions:

Step 1: Peel and cube the sweet potatoes. Remove stems from kale and chop the leaves.

Step 2: Heat olive oil in a large skillet or pot over medium heat. Add chopped onion and sauté for about 5 minutes until soft.

Step 3: Add chopped garlic and grated ginger, cooking for another 2 minutes until fragrant.

Step 4: Stir in curry powder, ground turmeric, and cumin seeds. Cook, stirring constantly, for 1 minute.

Step 5: Add the cubed sweet potatoes to the skillet, stirring to coat with the spices. Cook for 5 minutes.

Step 6: Pour in the coconut milk and vegetable broth. Bring to a simmer, then reduce heat to low and cover. Cook for 10-15 minutes until sweet potatoes are soft.

Step 7: Stir in chopped kale and cook for another 5 minutes until wilted.

Step 8: Season the curry with salt and black pepper.

Step 9: Garnish with fresh cilantro and serve hot with cooked rice or naan bread.

This vibrant curry blends the earthy sweetness of sweet potatoes with the bold spices of curry, creating a warming and nourishing meal.

Nutritional info (per serving): Cal 280 | Carb 42g | Fat 10g | Prot 6g | Fib 6g | Sugar 7g.

79. Butternut Squash and Sage Risotto

Preparation Time: 15 min. | Cooking Time: 40 min. | Servings: 4 | Difficulty: Medium.

Ingredients:

- Butternut squash, peeled, seeded, and cubed: 1 pound
- Arborio rice: 1 cup
- Vegetable broth: 1 quart
- Onion, finely chopped: 1 medium-sized
- Garlic, chopped: 2 cloves
- Fresh sage leaves, finely chopped: 8-10 leaves
- White wine: 1/2 cup
- Parmesan cheese, grated: 2 ounces
- Olive oil: 2 tablespoons
- Salt: 1 teaspoon
- Black pepper: 1/2 teaspoon
- Butter: 2 tablespoons

Instructions:

Step 1: Peel, seed, and cube the butternut squash.

Step 2: In a pot, heat the vegetable broth over medium heat until simmering. Reduce the heat to low to keep it warm.

Step 3: In a large skillet or pot, heat the olive oil over medium heat. Add the chopped onion and sauté for about 3-4 minutes until translucent.

Step 4: Add the chopped garlic and sage leaves to the skillet and cook for another 2 minutes until fragrant.

Step 5: Stir in the Arborio rice, ensuring it's well-coated with the onion mixture. Cook for 2-3 minutes until the rice is slightly toasted.

Step 6: Pour in the white wine and cook, stirring frequently, until absorbed by the rice.

Step 7: Gradually add the warm vegetable broth one ladle at a time, stirring often. Allow the rice to absorb the broth before adding more. Continue cooking until the rice is creamy and soft, about 20-25 minutes.

Step 8: In the last 10 minutes of cooking, add the cubed butternut squash to the risotto and continue to cook until the squash is tender and the rice is fully cooked.

Step 9: Stir in the grated Parmesan and butter until melted and creamy.

Step 10: Season with salt and black pepper to taste.

Step 11: Serve the butternut squash and sage risotto on plates.

Step 12: Garnish with additional chopped sage leaves and grated Parmesan if desired.

Step 13: Serve hot and enjoy!

The combination of creamy risotto, sweet squash, and fragrant sage makes for a satisfying meal that's perfect for any occasion. A warm and nourishing dish that combines rich flavors and textures.

Nutritional info (per serving): Cal 380 | Carb 60g | Fat 10g | Prot 10g | Fib 7g | Sugar 10g.

80. Eggplant and Chickpea Tagine

Preparation Time: 15 min.| Cooking Time: 40 min. | Servings: 4 | Difficulty: Medium.

Ingredients:

- Eggplant, cubed: 1 large (about 1 pound)

- Chickpeas, drained and rinsed: 1 can (15 oz)
- Onion, finely chopped: 1 large
- Garlic, finely chopped: 3 cloves
- Tomato, diced: 2 medium
- Tomato paste: 2 tablespoons
- Vegetable broth: 1 cup
- Ground cumin: 1 teaspoon
- Ground coriander: 1 teaspoon
- Ground paprika: 1/2 teaspoon
- Ground cinnamon: 1/2 teaspoon
- Ground turmeric: 1/2 teaspoon
- Salt: 1 teaspoon or to taste
- Black pepper: 1/2 teaspoon or to preference
- Olive oil: 2 tablespoons
- Fresh coriander: for garnishing
- Cooked couscous or rice: for serving

Instructions:

Step 1: Cube the eggplant.

Step 2: Finely chop the onion and garlic and dice the tomatoes.

Step 3: Heat olive oil in a large skillet or a tagine pot over medium heat.

Step 4: Add chopped onion and garlic to the skillet. Cook for about 3-4 minutes until soft and fragrant.

Step 5: Add eggplant cubes to the skillet and sauté for another 5 minutes until slightly browned.

Step 6: Stir in diced tomatoes, tomato paste, and drained chickpeas.

Step 7: Add ground cumin, ground coriander, ground paprika, ground cinnamon, and ground turmeric to the skillet. Stir well to combine all ingredients.

Step 8: Pour in the vegetable broth and bring the mixture to a simmer. Reduce heat to low, cover, and simmer for about 20-25 minutes, stirring occasionally, until the eggplant is tender and flavors have melded.

Step 9: Season with salt and black pepper to taste.

Step 10: Serve the eggplant and chickpea tagine hot, garnished with fresh coriander.

Step 11: Serve with cooked couscous or rice as preferred.

This tagine combines a variety of spices to create deep, earthy flavors that will warm and nourish you. It's the perfect combination of healthful ingredients and satisfying taste.

Nutritional info (per serving): Cal 280 | Carb 45g | Fat 7g | Prot 10g | Fib 8g | Sugar 10g.

81. Stuffed Bell Peppers with Quinoa and Vegetables

Preparation Time: 20 min. | Cooking Time: 40 min. | Servings: 4 | Difficulty: Easy.

Ingredients:

- Bell peppers: 4 large
- Quinoa, rinsed: 1 cup
- Vegetable broth: 2 cups
- Onion, finely chopped: 1 medium
- Carrot, diced: 1 medium
- Zucchini, diced: 1 medium
- Tomato, diced: 1 large
- Garlic, chopped: 2 cloves
- Tomato paste: 2 tablespoons
- Paprika: 1 teaspoon
- Dried oregano: 1 teaspoon
- Salt: 1/2 teaspoon or to taste
- Black pepper: 1/4 teaspoon or to taste
- Olive oil: 2 tablespoons
- Grated cheese (optional): for sprinkling

Instructions:

Step 1: Preheat the oven to 190°C (375°F).

Step 2: Remove the tops of the bell peppers and clear out the seeds and membranes. Set aside.

Step 3: Rinse the quinoa under cold water until the water runs clear.

Step 4: Finely chop the onion and garlic and dice the carrot, zucchini, and tomato.

Step 5: In a medium pot, bring the vegetable broth to a boil.

Step 6: Stir in the rinsed quinoa, reduce heat, cover, and simmer for 15-20 minutes until the quinoa is cooked and the liquid is absorbed.

Step 7: Heat olive oil in a large skillet over medium heat.

Step 8: Add chopped onion and garlic to the skillet. Cook until soft and fragrant, about 3-4 minutes.

Step 9: Stir in the diced carrot and cook for 2-3 minutes.

Step 10: Add zucchini cubes and cook for another 2-3 minutes.

Step 11: Stir in diced tomato, tomato paste, paprika, dried oregano, salt, and black pepper. Cook for another 2-3 minutes.

Step 12: Remove the skillet from heat and stir in the cooked quinoa until everything is well combined.

Step 13: Stuff each bell pepper with the quinoa-vegetable mixture, pressing down lightly to compact the filling.

Step 14: Place the stuffed bell peppers upright in a baking dish.

Step 15: Cover the dish with foil and bake in the preheated oven for 25-30 minutes until the bell peppers are tender.

Step 16: Remove the foil and sprinkle each stuffed pepper with grated cheese, if desired.

Step 17: Return the dish to the oven and bake for another 5 minutes or until the cheese is melted and bubbly.

Step 18: Serve the stuffed bell peppers hot, garnished with fresh herbs if desired.

These stuffed bell peppers are packed with a delicious quinoa and vegetable filling, making them a hearty and nutritious meal perfect for any time of the day.

Nutritional info (per serving): Cal 290 | Carb 49g | Fat 7g | Prot 9g | Fib 8g | Sugar 7g.
290, Fat 7g, Carbohydrates 49g, Protein 9g

82. Stir-Fried Vegetables and Tofu

Preparation Time: 15 min. | Cooking Time: 15 min. | Servings: 4 | Difficulty: Easy.

Ingredients:

- Firm tofu, drained and cubed: 14 oz
- Broccoli, cut into florets: 1 small head
- Carrots, julienned: 2 medium
- Bell peppers (various colors), sliced: 2 medium
- Sugar snap peas, trimmed: 7 oz
- Onion, sliced: 1 medium
- Garlic, chopped: 3 cloves
- Ginger, grated: 1 tablespoon
- Soy sauce: 3 tablespoons
- Sesame oil: 1 tablespoon
- Rice vinegar: 2 tablespoons
- Cornstarch: 1 tablespoon
- Water: 1/4 cup
- Olive oil: 2 tablespoons
- Salt: to taste
- Black pepper: to taste
- Cooked rice or noodles: for serving

Instructions:

Step 1: Drain the tofu and pat dry with paper towels.

Step 2: Cut the tofu into cubes and set aside.

Step 3: In a small bowl, mix soy sauce, rice vinegar, sesame oil, chopped garlic, grated ginger, cornstarch, and water. Set aside.

Step 4: Heat olive oil in a large pan or wok over medium-high heat.

Step 5: Add tofu cubes to the pan and fry until golden on all sides, about 5-7 minutes. Remove from the pan and set aside.

Step 6: If needed, add a bit more oil to the same pan, then add the sliced onion and cook for about 2-3 minutes until translucent.

Step 7: Add the sliced carrots, bell peppers, broccoli florets, and sugar snap peas to the pan. Stir-fry for 5-7 minutes until the vegetables are tender yet crisp.

Step 8: Return the cooked tofu to the pan with the vegetables.

Step 9: Briefly stir the sauce mixture, then pour it over the tofu and vegetables in the pan.

Step 10: Cook, stirring constantly, until the sauce thickens and coats the tofu and vegetables, about 2-3 minutes.

Step 11: Remove from heat and season with salt and black pepper.

Step 12: Serve the vegetable and tofu stir-fry hot with cooked rice or noodles.

This vibrant stir-fry combines tofu with colorful vegetables and a flavorful sauce, offering a nutritious and satisfying meal that's both light and filling.

Nutritional info (per serving): Cal 280 | Carb 30g | Fat 12g | Prot 15g | Fib 6g | Sugar 7g.

83. Stuffed Shells with Spinach and Ricotta

Preparation Time: 20 min. | Cooking Time: 30 min. | Servings: 4 | Difficulty: Medium.

Ingredients:

- Jumbo pasta shells: 8 oz
- Frozen spinach, thawed and drained: 7 oz
- Ricotta cheese: 15 oz
- Mozzarella cheese, shredded: 2 cups
- Parmesan cheese, grated: 1/2 cup
- Egg, beaten: 1
- Garlic, chopped: 2 cloves
- Dried oregano: 1 teaspoon
- Dried basil: 1 teaspoon
- Salt: 1/2 teaspoon
- Black pepper: 1/4 teaspoon
- Marinara sauce: 2 cups
- Olive oil: 2 tablespoons

Instructions:

Step 1: Cook the jumbo pasta shells to al dente according to package instructions.

Step 2: Drain the cooked shells and set aside to cool.

Step 3: In a large mixing bowl, combine the thawed and drained spinach, ricotta, shredded mozzarella, grated parmesan, beaten egg, chopped garlic, dried oregano, dried basil, salt, and black pepper. Mix well until all ingredients are evenly incorporated.

Step 4: Preheat the oven to 180°C (350°F).

Step 5: Generously fill each cooked pasta shell with the spinach-ricotta mixture, ensuring they are completely filled.

Step 6: Place the stuffed shells in a baking dish in a single layer.

Step 7: Pour the marinara sauce evenly over the stuffed shells in the baking dish.

Step 8: Drizzle olive oil over the top.

Step 9: Cover the baking dish with aluminum foil and bake in the preheated oven for 25-30 minutes, until the filling is heated through and the sauce is bubbling.

Step 10: After baking, remove the foil from the baking dish and optionally sprinkle additional grated parmesan over the top.

Step 11: Serve the stuffed shells with spinach and ricotta hot, garnished with fresh basil leaves if available.

These stuffed shells are a comforting, hearty dish, with creamy spinach and ricotta filling wrapped in soft pasta, all smothered in marinara sauce. They're perfect for a satisfying meal that's both flavorful and nourishing.

Nutritional info (per serving): Cal 450 | Carb 40g | Fat 20g | Prot 25g | Fib 4g | Sugar 7g.

84. Buddha Bowl with Chickpeas and Sweet Potatoes

Preparation Time: 15 min. | Cooking Time: 25 min. | Servings: 2 | Difficulty: Easy.

Ingredients:

- Sweet potatoes, peeled and cubed: 14 oz
- Chickpeas, drained and rinsed: 1 can (15 oz)
- Baby spinach: 4 cups
- Quinoa, uncooked: 1 cup
- Red onion, thinly sliced: 1 small
- Cherry tomatoes, halved: 1 1/2 cups
- Avocado, sliced: 1
- Olive oil: 2 tablespoons

- Paprika: 1 teaspoon
- Cumin: 1 teaspoon
- Garlic powder: 1/2 teaspoon
- Salt: 1/2 teaspoon
- Black pepper: 1/4 teaspoon
- Lemon, juiced: 1
- Tahini: 2 tablespoons
- Water: 2-4 tablespoons, as needed

Instructions:

Step 1: Preheat the oven to 200°C (400°F).

Step 2: Place the cubed sweet potatoes and drained chickpeas on a baking sheet.

Step 3: Drizzle with 1 tablespoon of olive oil and sprinkle with paprika, cumin, garlic powder, salt, and black pepper. Toss to coat evenly.

Step 4: Roast in the preheated oven for 20-25 minutes until the sweet potatoes are soft and the chickpeas are crispy.

Step 5: Rinse the quinoa under cold water.

Step 6: In a pot, combine the quinoa with 2 cups of water and a pinch of salt.

Step 7: Bring to a boil, then reduce heat and simmer covered for 15 minutes until the quinoa is cooked and the water is absorbed. Remove from heat and let it sit covered for 5 minutes. Fluff with a fork.

Step 8: Distribute the cooked quinoa, roasted sweet potatoes, roasted chickpeas, baby spinach, sliced red onions, cherry tomatoes, and avocado slices evenly between two serving bowls.

Step 9: In a small bowl, whisk together the remaining 1 tablespoon of olive oil, lemon juice, tahini, and water until smooth. Add more water as needed to achieve the desired consistency.

Step 10: Drizzle the tahini dressing over the assembled Buddha bowls.

Step 11: Garnish with additional black pepper and fresh herbs if desired.

Step 12: Serve immediately and enjoy!

This vibrant Buddha bowl combines roasted sweet potatoes, crispy chickpeas, and creamy avocado with a tangy tahini dressing. A wholesome, nutrient-packed meal that's as delicious as it is satisfying.

Nutritional info (per serving): Cal 550 | Carb 75g | Fat 20g | Prot 18g | Fib 12g | Sugar 12g.

85. Zucchini Lasagna with Cashew Ricotta

Preparation Time: 30 min. | Cooking Time: 45 min. | Servings: 4 | Difficulty: Medium.

Ingredients:

- Zucchini: 4 medium-sized
- Olive oil: 2 tablespoons
- Onion, chopped: 1
- Garlic, minced: 3 cloves
- Crushed tomatoes: 1 can
- Tomato paste: 2 tablespoons
- Fresh basil leaves, chopped: 1/2 cup
- Salt: 1 teaspoon
- Black pepper: 1/2 teaspoon
- Cashew nuts, soaked for 4 hours: 1 cup
- Lemon juice: 2 tablespoons
- Nutritional yeast: 2 tablespoons
- Garlic powder: 1/2 teaspoon
- Dried oregano: 1 teaspoon
- Baby spinach: 2 cups
- Vegan mozzarella cheese, shredded (optional): 1 cup

Instructions:

Step 1: Preheat the oven to 180°C (350°F).

Step 2: Slice the zucchini lengthwise into thin strips using a mandoline slicer or a sharp knife.

Step 3: Heat 1 tablespoon of olive oil in a large skillet over medium heat.

Step 4: Add the chopped onion and minced garlic. Cook until soft, about 5 minutes.

Step 5: Stir in the crushed tomatoes, tomato paste, chopped basil, salt, and black pepper. Simmer for 10-15 minutes, stirring occasionally, until the sauce thickens.

Step 6: Drain the soaked cashews and place them in a food processor.

Step 7: Add lemon juice, nutritional yeast, garlic powder, and dried oregano. Blend until smooth and creamy, scraping down the sides as needed.

Step 8: Spread a thin layer of tomato sauce at the bottom of a baking dish.

Step 9: Arrange a layer of zucchini slices over the sauce, followed by a layer of baby spinach.

Step 10: Dollop cashew ricotta over the spinach layer and spread evenly.

Step 11: Repeat the layers until all ingredients are used, ending with a layer of tomato sauce.

Step 12: Optionally, sprinkle shredded vegan mozzarella cheese over the top layer.

Step 13: Cover the baking dish with foil and bake in the preheated oven for 30 minutes.

Step 14: Remove the foil and bake for another 15 minutes or until the zucchini is tender and the cheese is melted and bubbly.

Step 15: Let the lasagna cool for a few minutes before slicing and serving.

Step 16: Garnish with fresh basil leaves if desired.

Step 17: Serve hot and enjoy!

This zucchini lasagna is a healthier, plant-based alternative to the classic dish, packed with fresh flavors and creamy cashew ricotta. A delicious and satisfying meal for any occasion.

Nutritional info (per serving): Cal 380 | Carb 35g | Fat 20g | Prot 15g | Fib 6g | Sugar 10g.

86. Vegetarian Shepherd's Pie with Lentils

Preparation Time: 20 min. | Cooking Time: 40 min. | Servings: 4 | Difficulty: Medium.

Ingredients:
- Brown lentils, dry: 1 cup
- Vegetable broth: 2 cups
- Olive oil: 2 tablespoons
- Onion, diced: 1
- Carrots, diced: 2
- Celery stalks, diced: 2
- Garlic, minced: 3 cloves
- Tomato paste: 2 tablespoons
- Frozen peas: 1 cup
- Corn kernels: 1 cup
- Fresh thyme leaves, chopped: 1 tablespoon
- Salt: 1 teaspoon
- Black pepper: 1/2 teaspoon
- Potatoes, peeled and diced: 4 medium-sized
- Butter or vegan butter: 2 tablespoons
- Milk or plant-based milk: 1/4 cup
- Nutmeg: 1/4 teaspoon
- Parmesan cheese or nutritional yeast (optional), grated: 1/4 cup

Instructions:
Step 1: Rinse and drain the brown lentils under cold water.

Step 2: In a pot, combine the lentils and vegetable broth. Bring to a boil, then reduce heat and simmer for 20-25 minutes until the lentils are tender and most of the broth has been absorbed.

Step 3: Heat the olive oil in a large skillet over medium heat.

Step 4: Add the chopped onion, diced carrots, and diced celery. Cook until the vegetables are soft, about 5-7 minutes.

Step 5: Add the minced garlic and cook for another minute.

Step 6: Stir in the tomato paste, frozen peas, corn kernels, chopped thyme leaves, salt, and black pepper. Cook for another 5 minutes, then remove from heat.

Step 7: Place the diced potatoes in a pot of salted water. Bring to a boil and cook until the potatoes are fork-tender, about 15-20 minutes.

Step 8: Drain the potatoes and return them to the pot.

Step 9: Add butter (or vegan butter), milk (or plant-based milk), and nutmeg to the pot. Mash the potatoes until smooth and creamy. Season with salt and pepper to taste.

Step 10: Preheat the oven to 200°C (400°F).

Step 11: Spread the lentil filling in a baking dish and even it out.

Step 12: Spoon the mashed potatoes over the lentil filling and smooth it out with a spatula.

Step 13: Optionally, sprinkle grated Parmesan cheese or nutritional yeast over the top to enrich the flavor.

Step 14: Bake in the preheated oven for 20-25 minutes until the top is golden brown and the filling bubbles around the edges.

Step 15: Let the shepherd's pie cool for a few minutes before serving.

Step 16: Garnish with fresh thyme leaves if desired.

Step 17: Serve hot and enjoy!

This hearty vegetarian shepherd's pie with lentils and vegetables is a comforting, wholesome meal perfect for any occasion. A satisfying dish that's full of flavor and nutrients.

Nutritional info (per serving): Cal 420 | Carb 70g | Fat 8g | Prot 17g | Fib 12g | Sugar 7g.

87. CAULIFLOWER AND CHICKPEA COCONUT CURRY

Preparation Time: 10 min. | Cooking Time: 30 min. | Servings: 4 | Difficulty: Medium.

Ingredients:

- Cauliflower florets: 4 cups
- Canned chickpeas, drained and rinsed: 1 can (15 oz)
- Coconut milk (light): 1 cup
- Vegetable broth: 1/2 cup
- Onion, finely chopped: 1
- Garlic cloves, minced: 2
- Fresh ginger, grated: 1 teaspoon
- Ground turmeric: 1 teaspoon
- Ground cumin: 1 teaspoon
- Ground coriander: 1/2 teaspoon
- Olive oil: 1 tablespoon
- Fresh spinach: 2 cups
- Lime juice: 1 tablespoon
- Fresh cilantro, chopped: for garnish

Instructions:

Step 1: Heat olive oil in a large pan over medium heat. Add the onion and sauté for 5 minutes until softened.

Step 2: Add the minced garlic and grated ginger, and cook for another 1-2 minutes until fragrant.

Step 3: Stir in the turmeric, cumin, and coriander, cooking for 30 seconds to release the flavors.

Step 4: Add the cauliflower florets and chickpeas, stirring to coat them evenly with the spices.

Step 5: Pour in the coconut milk and vegetable broth, stirring well. Bring to a gentle simmer.

Step 6: Cover the pan and let it cook for 15-20 minutes, or until the cauliflower is tender.

Step 7: Add the fresh spinach and stir until wilted. Finish with lime juice for brightness.

Step 8: Serve warm, garnished with chopped cilantro.

This cauliflower and chickpea coconut curry is rich in flavor and nutrients, providing plant-based protein and anti-inflammatory benefits. It's a comforting dish that perfectly supports a healthy liver.

Nutritional info (per serving): Cal 280 | Carb 32g | Fat 12g | Prot 9g | Fib 8g | Sugar 7g.

Chapter 8: Dessert

Indulge in Sweet Treats Without Sacrificing Health

———— ❖ ————

88. Baked Apples with Cinnamon and Nuts

Preparation Time: 10 min. | Cooking Time: 30 min. | Servings: 2 | Difficulty: Easy.

Ingredients:

- Apples (such as Granny Smith or Gala): 2 large
- Ground cinnamon: 1 teaspoon
- Chopped nuts (e.g., walnuts or almonds): 1/4 cup
- Maple syrup or honey: 2 tablespoons
- Rolled oats: 2 tablespoons
- Unsweetened applesauce: 2 tablespoons
- Melted coconut oil or butter: 1 tablespoon

Instructions:

Step 1: Preheat your oven to 350°F (180°C).

Step 2: Wash the apples and slice off the top end. Core the apples to create a well in the center, making sure not to puncture through the bottom.

Step 3: In a small bowl, combine the chopped nuts, ground cinnamon, maple syrup or honey, rolled oats, and unsweetened applesauce until well mixed.

Step 4: Fill each apple with the nut mixture, pressing down slightly to compact it.

Step 5: Place the stuffed apples in a baking dish. Drizzle each apple with the melted coconut oil or butter.

Step 6: Bake in the preheated oven for 25-30 minutes, until the apples are soft and the filling is golden brown.

Step 7: Remove the baked apples from the oven and let them cool for a few minutes before serving.

Step 8: Serve the baked apples warm, optionally topped with a dollop of yogurt or a sprinkle of extra cinnamon if desired.

These warm, cinnamon-scented baked apples are a comforting, healthy treat that's perfect for satisfying your sweet tooth with wholesome ingredients.

Nutritional info (per serving): Cal 250 | Carb 40g | Fat 10g | Protein 3g | Fiber 5g | Sugar 30g.

89. Avocado Chocolate Mousse

Preparation Time: 10 min. | Cooking Time: 30 min. | Servings: 2 | Difficulty: Easy.

Ingredients:

- Ripe avocados: 2 medium-sized
- Unsweetened cocoa powder: 4 tablespoons

- Maple syrup or honey: 4 tablespoons
- Vanilla extract: 1 teaspoon
- Almond milk or milk of choice: 1/4 cup
- Fresh berries or sliced fruit for garnishing (optional)

Instructions:

Step 1: Halve the avocados, remove the pits and scoop the flesh into a blender or food processor.

Step 2: Add the cocoa powder, maple syrup or honey, vanilla extract, and almond milk to the blender.

Step 3: Blend until smooth and creamy. Stop as needed to scrape down the sides of the blender to ensure everything is well incorporated.

Step 4: Taste the mousse and adjust the sweetness if necessary by adding more maple syrup or honey.

Step 5: For a firmer consistency, you can chill the mousse in the refrigerator for about 30 minutes before serving.

Step 6: Distribute the avocado chocolate mousse into glasses or bowls.

Step 7: Garnish with fresh berries or sliced fruit if desired.

Step 8: Serve immediately and enjoy!

This creamy avocado chocolate mousse is rich, indulgent, and guilt-free, making it a perfect treat for those seeking a healthier dessert option.

Nutritional info (per serving): Cal 280 | Carb 28g | Fat 20g | Prot 5g | Fib 8g | Sugar 15g.

90. CHIA SEEDS AND BERRY PUDDING

Preparation Time: 5 min. | Cooking Time: 0 min. | Servings: 2 | Difficulty: Easy.

Ingredients:
- Chia seeds: 1/3 cup

- Unsweetened almond milk: 2 cups
- Fresh mixed berries (e.g., strawberries, blueberries, raspberries): 1 cup
- Maple syrup or honey (optional): 2 tablespoons
- Vanilla extract: 1 teaspoon

Instructions:

Step 1: In a mixing bowl, combine chia seeds, unsweetened almond milk, maple syrup or honey (if using), and vanilla extract. Stir well to ensure the chia seeds are evenly distributed.

Step 2: Cover the bowl and refrigerate the chia seed mixture for at least 2 hours or ideally overnight, to allow the chia seeds to absorb the liquid and thicken.

Step 3: Warm the mixed berries in a saucepan over medium heat. If desired, add a splash of water or lemon juice to help release the juices. Cook for 5-7 minutes until the berries are soft and have released their juices, stirring occasionally.

Step 4: Evenly distribute the chilled chia seed mixture into serving bowls or glasses.

Step 5: Top each serving with the warm berry compote.

Step 6: Serve the chia seed and berry pudding immediately, garnished with additional fresh berries or a drizzle of honey if desired.

This creamy chia pudding blends the natural sweetness of berries with a light, satisfying texture, making it perfect as a nourishing breakfast or a guilt-free dessert.

Nutritional info (per serving): Cal 250 | Carb 30g | Fat 8g | Prot 5g | Fib 10g | Sugar 10g.

91. ALMOND FLOUR LEMON BARS

Preparation Time: 15 min. | Cooking Time: 25 min. | Servings: 4 | Difficulty: Easy.

Ingredients:

- Almond flour: 2 cups
- Butter, melted: 1/3 cup
- Erythritol powder or sweetener of choice: 1/3 cup
- Salt: 1/4 teaspoon
- Eggs: 2
- Lemon juice: 1/2 cup (about 4 lemons)
- Zest from lemons: from 2 lemons
- Baking powder: 1/2 teaspoon
- Erythritol powder or sweetener of choice for dusting (optional)

Instructions:

Step 1: Preheat the oven to 180°C (350°F) and line a baking dish with parchment paper.

Step 2: In a mixing bowl, combine almond flour, melted butter, erythritol or powdered sweetener, and salt. Mix until well combined.

Step 3: Press the mixture evenly into the bottom of the prepared baking dish to form a crust.

Step 4: Bake the crust in the preheated oven for 10-12 minutes until lightly golden, then remove and allow to cool slightly.

Step 5: In another mixing bowl, whisk together the eggs, lemon juice, lemon zest, baking powder, and erythritol or sweetener powder until smooth.

Step 6: Pour the lemon filling over the partially baked crust and spread evenly.

Step 7: Return the baking dish to the oven and bake for 12-15 minutes until the filling is set and the edges are slightly golden.

Step 8: Let the lemon bars cool completely in the baking dish before cutting into squares.

Step 9: Optionally, dust the bars with erythritol powder or sweetener before serving.

These bright and tangy lemon bars pair a nutty almond flour crust with a zesty citrus filling, creating a refreshing dessert that's both light and satisfying.

Nutritional info (per serving): Cal 280 | Carb 12g | Fat 22g | Prot 8g | Fib 4g | Sugar 5g.

92. Coconut and Mango Rice Pudding

Preparation Time: 10 min. | Cooking Time: 30 min. | Servings: 4 | Difficulty: Easy.

Ingredients:

- Arborio rice: 3/4 cup
- Coconut milk: 1 3/4 cups
- Water: 3/4 cup
- Sugar (or sweetener of choice): 1/4 cup
- Ripe mango, diced: 1
- Vanilla extract: 1 teaspoon
- Toasted coconut flakes: 1/4 cup (for garnish)
- Fresh mint leaves: for garnishing (optional)

Instructions:

Step 1: In a medium-sized saucepan, combine the Arborio rice, coconut milk, water, and sugar (or sweetener). Stir well until everything is well mixed.

Step 2: Bring the mixture to a boil over medium heat, then reduce the heat to low. Let it simmer uncovered, stirring occasionally, for about 25-30 minutes until the rice is tender and the mixture has thickened.

Step 3: While the rice is cooking, peel and dice the ripe mango.

Step 4: Once the rice is cooked and has reached the desired consistency, stir in the vanilla extract and diced mango. Mix well.

Step 5: Remove the rice pudding from the heat and allow it to cool slightly.

Step 6: Distribute the rice pudding into serving bowls.

Step 7: Garnish each serving with toasted coconut flakes and fresh mint leaves, if desired.

This creamy coconut and mango rice pudding marries tropical sweetness with a velvety texture, delivering a comforting yet exotic dessert that feels both indulgent and refreshing.

Nutritional info (per serving): Cal 290 | Carb 40g | Fat 12g | Prot 4g | Fib 3g | Sugar 15g.

93. Carrot Walnut Cake with Yogurt Frosting

Preparation Time: 20 min. | Cooking Time: 35 min. | Servings: 8 | Difficulty: Medium.

Ingredients:

- Carrots, grated: 2 cups
- Whole wheat flour: 1 3/4 cups
- Baking powder: 2 teaspoons
- Baking soda: 1 teaspoon
- Ground cinnamon: 1 teaspoon
- Ground nutmeg: 1/2 teaspoon
- Eggs: 3
- Unsweetened applesauce: 1/2 cup
- Honey or maple syrup: 1/2 cup
- Vanilla extract: 1 teaspoon
- Walnuts, chopped: 1 cup
For the Yogurt Frosting:
- Greek yogurt: 1 cup
- Honey or maple syrup: 2 tablespoons
- Lemon zest: 1 teaspoon

Instructions:

Step 1: Preheat the oven to 180°C (350°F).

Step 2: Grease and flour a round cake pan.

Step 3: In a large mixing bowl, combine the grated carrots, whole wheat flour, baking powder, baking soda, ground cinnamon, and ground nutmeg. Mix well.

Step 4: In another bowl, whisk together the eggs, applesauce, honey or maple syrup, and vanilla extract until well combined.

Step 5: Gradually add the wet ingredients to the dry ingredients, stirring until just combined.

Step 6: Fold in the chopped walnuts.

Step 7: Pour the batter into the prepared cake pan and spread evenly.

Step 8: Bake in the preheated oven for 30-35 min. or until a toothpick inserted into the center comes out clean.

Step 9: Remove the cake from the oven and let it cool completely before frosting.

Step 10: In a small bowl, whisk together the Greek yogurt, honey or maple syrup, and lemon zest until smooth.

Step 11: Once the cake has cooled, spread the yogurt frosting evenly over the cake.

Step 12: Slice and serve.

This fragrant carrot walnut cake combines wholesome ingredients and warm spices, resulting in a moist, flavorful treat. The tangy yogurt frosting adds a perfect balance, making it an ideal choice for any occasion.

Nutritional info (per serving): Cal 280 | Carb 42g | Fat 10g | Prot 8g | Fib 5g | Sugar 5g.

94. Oatmeal Banana Cookies

Preparation Time: 10 min. | Baking Time: 15 min. | Servings: 12 | Difficulty: Easy.

Ingredients:

- Oats: 1 1/2 cups
- Ripe bananas, pureed: 2
- Almond butter or peanut butter: 1/3 cup
- Honey or maple syrup: 2 tablespoons
- Vanilla extract: 1 teaspoon
- Ground cinnamon: 1 teaspoon
- Baking powder: 1/2 teaspoon
- Dark chocolate chips (optional): 1/3 cup
- Chopped nuts (such as walnuts or almonds) (optional): 1/2 cup

Instructions:

Step 1: Preheat the oven to 180°C (350°F). Line a baking sheet with parchment paper.

Step 2: In a large mixing bowl, combine the mashed bananas, almond or peanut butter, honey or maple syrup, and vanilla extract. Mix well until smooth.

Step 3: Add the oats, ground cinnamon, and baking powder to the bowl. Stir until all ingredients are evenly mixed.

Step 4: If desired, fold in the dark chocolate chips and chopped nuts for added flavor.

Step 5: Take about 1-2 tablespoons of the cookie dough and place it on the prepared baking sheet. Flatten the cookies with your hands or the back of a spoon to form rounds.

Step 6: Place the baking sheet in the preheated oven and bake for 12-15 minutes or until the cookies are golden brown around the edges.

Step 7: Remove from the oven and let the cookies cool on the baking sheet for 5 minutes before transferring them to a wire rack to cool completely.

Step 8: Serve these delicious oatmeal banana cookies as a healthy snack or dessert after cooling.

These oatmeal banana cookies are soft, naturally sweetened, and packed with nutrients, making them a perfect choice for a quick and satisfying treat.

Nutritional info (per serving): Cal 120 | Carb 18g | Fat 5g | Prot 3g | Fib 2g | Sugar 4g.

95. Pumpkin Spice Energy Balls

Preparation Time: 15 min. | Cooking Time: 0 min. | Servings: 12 | Difficulty: Easy.

Ingredients:

- Oats: 1 1/2 cups
- Pumpkin puree: 1/2 cup
- Medjool dates, pitted: 1/2 cup
- Almond butter: 1/4 cup
- Chia seeds: 2 tablespoons
- Pumpkin pie spice: 2 teaspoons
- Vanilla extract: 1 teaspoon
- Maple syrup or honey: 2 tablespoons
- Coconut flakes, for rolling (optional): 1/3 cup

Instructions:

Step 1: If your dates are not soft, soak them in warm water for 10 minutes to soften. Drain before use.

Step 2: Combine oats, pumpkin puree, pitted dates, almond butter, chia seeds, pumpkin pie spice, vanilla extract, and maple syrup or honey in a food processor. Pulse until the mixture comes together and forms a sticky dough.

Step 3: Take tablespoon-sized portions of the dough and roll them into balls with your hands. If the dough is too sticky, you can slightly moisten your hands to prevent sticking.

Step 4: If desired, roll the balls in coconut flakes to enhance flavor and texture.

Step 5: Place the energy balls on a baking sheet lined with parchment paper and chill in the refrigerator for at least 30 minutes to set.

Step 6: Once chilled, the pumpkin spice energy balls are ready to be served. Leftovers can be stored in an airtight container in the refrigerator for up to a week.

These pumpkin spice energy balls are quick to prepare and loaded with fiber and nutrients, making them a tasty and satisfying snack for liver health.

Nutritional info (per serving): Cal 110 | Carb 17g | Fat 4g | Prot 2g | Fib 3g | Sugar 8g.

96. Baked Pears with Honey and Walnuts

Preparation Time: 10 min. | Cooking Time: 25 min. | Servings: 2 | Difficulty: Easy.

Ingredients:
- Pears (firm but ripe): 2
- Chopped walnuts: 1/4 cup
- Honey: 2 tablespoons
- Ground cinnamon: 1/2 teaspoon
- Lemon juice: 1 tablespoon

Instructions:
Step 1: Preheat your oven to 180°C (350°F).
Step 2: Wash and dry the pears. Cut the pears in half lengthwise and use a spoon to scoop out the core and seeds, creating a cavity.
Step 3: In a small bowl, mix the chopped walnuts, honey, ground cinnamon, and lemon juice until well combined.
Step 4: Place the pear halves cut-side up in a baking dish. Evenly fill the hollowed-out pear halves with

the walnut mixture, pressing gently to compact the filling.

Step 5: Bake in the preheated oven for about 20-25 minutes, until the pears are soft and the topping is golden brown and caramelized.

Step 6: Remove the pears from the oven and let them cool slightly. Serve warm, optionally with a scoop of vanilla ice cream or a dollop of Greek yogurt.

These baked pears are a naturally sweet and nutritious dessert, rich in fiber and healthy fats. Perfect for a liver-friendly diet, they offer a warm and satisfying treat.

Nutritional info (per serving): Cal 220 | Carb 32g | Fat 10g | Prot 2g | Fib 4g | Sugar 22g.

97. Dark Chocolate and Almond Bark

Preparation Time: 10 min. | Cooking Time: 10 min. | Servings: 4 | Difficulty: Easy.

Ingredients:
- Dark chocolate (70% cocoa or higher), chopped: 7 oz
- Almonds, chopped: 1/2 cup
- Sea salt flakes (optional): 1/4 teaspoon

Instructions:
Step 1: Melt the dark chocolate in a heatproof bowl set over a pot of boiling water, stirring occasionally until the chocolate is smooth and fully melted.
Step 2: While the chocolate is melting, evenly spread the chopped almonds on a baking sheet lined with parchment paper.
Step 3: Once the chocolate has melted, pour it over the chopped almonds on the baking sheet. Use a

spatula to spread the chocolate evenly, ensuring all almonds are covered.

Step 4: If desired, sprinkle the sea salt flakes evenly over the melted chocolate and almonds to create a sweet and savory contrast.

Step 5: Allow the chocolate bark to set at room temperature for about 10 minutes. Alternatively, you can place it in the refrigerator to set more quickly.

Step 6: Once the chocolate has hardened, break it into small, irregular pieces with your hands or a knife.

Step 7: Serve the dark chocolate and almond bark immediately or store it in an airtight container in the refrigerator for up to a week.

This dark chocolate and almond bark is a quick, delicious treat that balances healthy fats with antioxidants, making it both nutritious and satisfying. The hint of sea salt adds a delightful flavor twist perfect for mindful indulgence.

Nutritional info (per serving): Cal 250 | Carb 15g | Fat 18g | Prot 5g | Fib 4g | Sugar 10g.

98. Peach Raspberry Crisp

Preparation Time: 15 min. | Cooking Time: 40 min. | Servings: 4 | Difficulty: Medium.

Ingredients:

- Peaches, peeled, pitted, and sliced: 4 cups
- Raspberries: 1 cup
- Lemon juice: 1 tablespoon
- Granulated sugar: 1/4 cup
- Cornstarch: 1 tablespoon
- Rolled oats: 1 cup
- Almond flour: 1/2 cup
- Brown sugar: 1/4 cup
- Ground cinnamon: 1 teaspoon
- Unsalted butter, cold and cubed: 1/3 cup

Instructions:

Step 1: Preheat the oven to 180°C (350°F).

Step 2: In a bowl, mix the sliced peaches, raspberries, lemon juice, granulated sugar, and cornstarch. Gently toss to coat the fruits evenly with the sugar-cornstarch mixture.

Step 3: Transfer the fruit mixture to a 9x9-inch baking dish and spread it out evenly.

Step 4: In another bowl, combine the rolled oats, almond flour, brown sugar, and ground cinnamon. Mix well.

Step 5: Add the cubed cold butter and use your fingers to rub it into the dry ingredients until the mixture resembles coarse crumbs.

Step 6: Evenly sprinkle the crisp topping over the fruit mixture in the baking dish, ensuring it is completely covered.

Step 7: Place the baking dish in the preheated oven and bake for 35-40 minutes until the fruit is bubbling and the topping is golden brown.

Step 8: Remove from the oven and let cool for a few minutes before serving. Serve warm, optionally with a scoop of vanilla ice cream or a dollop of whipped cream.

This peach raspberry crisp combines sweet, juicy fruits with a crunchy oat topping, offering a delicious dessert full of fiber and natural flavors. It's quick to prepare and perfect for a healthier treat.

Nutritional info (per serving): Cal 320 | Carb 47g | Fat 14g | Prot 5g | Fib 6g | Sugar 22g.

99. Fig and Ricotta Toast

Preparation Time: 5 min. | Cooking Time: 0 min. | Servings: 2 | Difficulty: Easy.

Ingredients:

- Whole grain bread slices: 4 slices
- Ricotta cheese: 3/4 cup
- Fresh figs, sliced: 4
- Honey: 2 tablespoons
- Chopped pistachios: 2 tablespoons
- Fresh mint leaves: for garnishing (optional)

Instructions:

Step 1: If desired, toast the whole grain bread slices until golden brown.

Step 2: Spread an equal amount of ricotta cheese on each toasted bread slice.

Step 3: Place the sliced fresh figs on top of the ricotta cheese, distributing them evenly across the slices.

Step 4: Drizzle honey over the figs and ricotta on each toast, to taste.

Step 5: Sprinkle chopped pistachios over the figs and ricotta on each toast.

Step 6: Optionally, garnish with fresh mint leaves to add a touch of color and freshness. Serve immediately.

This fig and ricotta toast offers a creamy texture, natural sweetness, and a boost of nutrients, making it a quick, liver-friendly snack or light meal.

Nutritional info (per serving): Cal 260 | Carb 39g | Fat 8g | Prot 9g | Fib 4g | Sugar 18g.

100. LEMON YOGURT PARFAIT

Preparation Time: 10 min. | Cooking Time: 0 min. | Servings: 2 | Difficulty: Easy.

Ingredients:

- Low-fat Greek yogurt: 1 3/4 cups
- Fresh blueberries: 1 cup
- Honey: 2 tablespoons
- Lemon zest: From 1 lemon
- Granola: 1 cup

Instructions:

Step 1: In a mixing bowl, combine Greek yogurt, honey, and lemon zest. Stir well until the mixture is smooth and well combined.

Step 2: Start with a layer of the prepared yogurt mixture at the bottom of serving glasses or bowls.

Step 3: Add a layer of fresh blueberries on top of the yogurt mixture.

Step 4: Sprinkle a layer of granola over the blueberries.

Step 5: Repeat the layers until the glasses are filled, finishing with a granola layer on top.

Step 6: Optionally garnish the top layer with a few additional blueberries and some lemon zest.

Step 7: Serve immediately as a delicious and nutritious breakfast, snack, or dessert.

This lemon yogurt parfait combines creamy yogurt, fresh fruit, and crunchy granola, offering a balanced and refreshing treat that supports a healthy, liver-friendly diet.

Nutritional info (per serving): Cal 300 | Carb 48g | Fat 5g | Prot 15g | Fib 6g | Sugar 28g.

101. SPICED BAKED QUINOA PUDDING

Preparation Time: 10 min. | Cooking Time: 40 min. | Servings: 4 | Difficulty: Medium.

Ingredients:

- Quinoa: 1 cup
- Low-fat milk: 2 cups
- Maple syrup: 1/4 cup
- Vanilla extract: 1 teaspoon

- Ground cinnamon: 1 teaspoon
- Ground nutmeg: 1/4 teaspoon
- Ground ginger: 1/4 teaspoon
- Raisins: 1/4 cup
- Chopped walnuts: 1/4 cup

Instructions:

Step 1: Preheat the oven to 180°C (350°F).

Step 2: Rinse the quinoa in a fine mesh sieve under cold water.

Step 3: In a saucepan, combine the rinsed quinoa with the milk. Bring to a boil over medium heat.

Step 4: Reduce the heat to low, cover, and simmer for about 15 minutes, until the quinoa is cooked and most of the milk has been absorbed.

Step 5: In a mixing bowl, combine the cooked quinoa, maple syrup, vanilla extract, ground cinnamon, ground nutmeg, ground ginger, raisins, and chopped walnuts. Mix well.

Step 6: Transfer the quinoa mixture into a lightly greased baking dish.

Step 7: Bake in the preheated oven for 25-30 minutes, until the pudding is set and slightly golden on top.

Step 8: Serve the spiced baked quinoa pudding warm as a cozy and nutritious dessert or breakfast option.

This spiced quinoa pudding is a wholesome and satisfying dish, packed with protein and warming spices. It's a delicious and nutrient-dense option perfect for starting your day or ending a meal.

Nutritional info (per serving): Cal 300 | Carb 45g | Fat 8g | Prot 10g | Fib 5g | Sugar 18g.

102. Zucchini Brownies with Avocado Frosting

Preparation Time: 15 min. | Cooking Time: 30 min. | Servings: 4 | Difficulty: Medium.

Ingredients:

- Zucchini, grated: 2 cups
- Unsweetened applesauce: 1/2 cup
- Maple syrup: 1/2 cup
- Vanilla extract: 1 teaspoon
- Eggs: 2
- Almond flour: 1 cup
- Cocoa powder: 1/2 cup
- Baking soda: 1 teaspoon
- Salt: 1/4 teaspoon
- Dark chocolate chips: 1/2 cup
For the Avocado Frosting:
- Ripe avocado: 1
- Cocoa powder: 1/4 cup
- Maple syrup: 1/4 cup
- Vanilla extract: 1 teaspoon

Instructions:

Step 1: Preheat your oven to 180°C (350°F).

Step 2: Grease a baking dish or line it with parchment paper.

Step 3: In a large mixing bowl, combine the grated zucchini, unsweetened applesauce, maple syrup, vanilla extract, and eggs. Mix well.

Step 4: Add the almond flour, cocoa powder, baking soda, and salt to the zucchini mixture. Stir until well combined.

Step 5: Fold in the dark chocolate chips.

Step 6: Pour the batter into the prepared baking dish and spread evenly.

Step 7: Bake in the preheated oven for 25-30 minutes or until a toothpick inserted in the center comes out clean.

Step 8: Remove from the oven and let cool completely before frosting.

Step 9: In a food processor or blender, blend the ripe avocado, cocoa powder, maple syrup, and vanilla extract. Puree until smooth and creamy.

Step 10: Once the brownies have cooled, spread the avocado frosting evenly over the cake.

Step 11: Cut the brownies into squares and serve.

These zucchini brownies are rich, fudgy, and naturally sweetened, while the creamy avocado frosting adds healthy fats and a smooth finish. A perfect way to enjoy a nutritious, indulgent treat.

Nutritional info (per serving): Cal 350 | Carb 40g | Fat 18g | Prot 8g | Fib 6g | Sugar 20g.

Chapter 9: 4-Week Nutrition Plan

A Structured Guide to Stay on Track

———— ❖ ————

This great plan includes breakfast, lunch, dinner and dessert, focusing on a blend of flavors and nutrients to cater to various dietary needs and preferences.

Week 1

Day 1:

- Breakfast: Avocado and Egg Toast on Whole Grain Bread
- Lunch: Grilled Chicken and Avocado Salad
- Dinner: Savory Lentil and Kale Soup
- Dessert: Avocado Chocolate Mousse

Day 2:

- Breakfast: Oatmeal with Walnuts and Berries
- Lunch: Baked Cod with Lemon and Dill
- Dinner: Quinoa and Roasted Vegetable Salad
- Dessert: Baked Apples with Cinnamon and Nuts

Day 3:

- Breakfast: Chia Seed Pudding with Kiwi and Coconut
- Lunch: Turkey-Quinoa Meatballs with Tomato-Basil Sauce
- Dinner: Sweet Potato and Kale Curry
- Dessert: Lemon Yogurt Parfait

Day 4:

- Breakfast: Golden Turmeric Smoothie
- Lunch: Pan-Fried Lean Beef and Broccoli
- Dinner: Miso Vegetable Soup with Tofu
- Dessert: Coconut and Mango Rice Pudding

Day 5:

- Breakfast: Spinach Mushroom Egg Muffins

- Lunch: Grilled Salmon with Avocado Salsa
- Dinner: Kale, Apple, and Walnut Salad
- Dessert: Almond Flour Lemon Bars

Day 6:

- Breakfast: Quinoa Breakfast Bowl with Mixed Nuts and Seeds
- Lunch: Pork Tenderloin with Apple Cider Vinegar
- Dinner: Stuffed Portobello Mushrooms with Lentils and Spinach
- Dessert: Dark Chocolate and Almond Bark

Day 7:

- Breakfast: Beet and Berry Liver Smoothie
- Lunch: Spiced Beef Kabobs with Yogurt Sauce
- Dinner: Carrot Ginger Purée Soup
- Dessert: Peach Raspberry Crisp

WEEK 2

Day 1:

- Breakfast: Porridge Infused with Turmeric and Ginger
- Lunch: Baked Mediterranean Mackerel
- Dinner: Broccoli and Mixed Berries Detox Salad
- Dessert: Chia Seeds and Berry Pudding

Day 2:

- Breakfast: Kale and Sweet Potato Breakfast Salad
- Lunch: Pan-Fried Chicken and Vegetables
- Dinner: Butternut Squash and Sage Risotto
- Dessert: Carrot Walnut Cake with Yogurt Frosting

Day 3:

- Breakfast: Carrot-Ginger Smoothie
- Lunch: Spiralized Zoodles with Spicy Pork and Vegetables
- Dinner: Beetroot and Cabbage Healing Soup
- Dessert: Baked Pears with Honey and Walnuts

Day 4:

- Breakfast: Almond Butter and Banana on Sprouted Grain Toast

- Lunch: Steamed Trout in Asian Style
- Dinner: Stuffed Bell Peppers with Quinoa and Vegetables
- Dessert: Oatmeal Banana Cookies

Day 5:

- Breakfast: Pumpkin Spice Smoothie for the Liver
- Lunch: Beef with Balsamic Glaze and Roasted Vegetable Salad
- Dinner: Spicy Chickpea and Cucumber Salad
- Dessert: Zucchini Brownies with Avocado Frosting

Day 6:

- Breakfast: Zucchini and Carrot Fritters
- Lunch: Honey-Glazed Salmon with Quinoa Pilaf
- Dinner: Eggplant and Chickpea Tagine
- Dessert: Spiced Baked Quinoa Pudding

Day 7:

- Breakfast: Cucumber-Mint Refreshment Smoothie
- Lunch: Pork and Pineapple Skewers
- Dinner: Avocado and Grapefruit Salad
- Dessert: Fig and Ricotta Toast

WEEK 3

Day 1:

- Breakfast: Spicy Breakfast Bowl with Lentils and Vegetables
- Lunch: Stuffed Bell Peppers with Ground Beef and Quinoa
- Dinner: Quinoa and Black Bean Chili
- Dessert: Pumpkin Spice Energy Balls

Day 2:

- Breakfast: Greek Yogurt with Nuts, Seeds and Honey
- Lunch: Spicy Lime and Cilantro Tilapia
- Dinner: Sweet Potato and Spinach Salad
- Dessert: Baked Apples with Cinnamon and Nuts

Day 3:

- Breakfast: Liver-Cleansing Green Smoothie

- Lunch: Baked Lemon-Herb Chicken
- Dinner: Vegetarian Shepherd's Pie with Lentils
- Dessert: Almond Flour Lemon Bars

Day 4:
- Breakfast: Baked Sweet Potatoes and Avocado Hash
- Lunch: Curry Shrimp and Cauliflower Rice
- Dinner: Soothing Turmeric Chicken Soup
- Dessert: Dark Chocolate and Almond Bark

Day 5:
- Breakfast: Sweet Potato Pie Smoothie
- Lunch: Pan-Fried Lean Beef and Broccoli
- Dinner: Beetroot and Arugula Salad
- Dessert: Lemon Yogurt Parfait

Day 6:
- Breakfast: Smoked Salmon and Avocado Wrap
- Lunch: Asian-Inspired Turkey Salad Wraps
- Dinner: Stir-Fried Vegetables and Tofu
- Dessert: Chia Seeds and Berry Pudding

Day 7:
- Breakfast: Avocado Green Tea Smoothie
- Lunch: Beef and Sweet Potato Stew
- Dinner: Buddha Bowl with Chickpeas and Sweet Potatoes
- Dessert: Peach Raspberry Crisp

WEEK 4

Day 1:
- Breakfast: Spinach Mushroom Egg Muffins
- Lunch: Grilled Sardines with Pesto
- Dinner: Kale, Apple, and Walnut Salad
- Dessert: Avocado Chocolate Mousse

Day 2:
- Breakfast: Tropical Detox Smoothie

- Lunch: Pork Tenderloin in Herb Crust with Roasted Root Vegetables
- Dinner: Miso Vegetable Soup with Tofu
- Dessert: Zucchini Brownies with Avocado Frosting

Day 3:
- Breakfast: Chia Seed Omega Power Smoothie
- Lunch: Fish Tacos with Slaw
- Dinner: Stuffed Shells with Spinach and Ricotta
- Dessert: Carrot Walnut Cake with Yogurt Frosting

Day 4:
- Breakfast: Spicy Lemon-Apple Smoothie
- Lunch: Baked Cod with Lemon and Dill
- Dinner: Carrot Ginger Purée Soup
- Dessert: Pumpkin Spice Energy Balls

Day 5:
- Breakfast: Almond Butter Protein Kick Smoothie
- Lunch: Spiced Beef Kabobs with Yogurt Sauce
- Dinner: Broccoli and Mixed Berries Detox Salad
- Dessert: Lemon Yogurt Parfait

Day 6:
- Breakfast: Papaya Digestive Smoothie
- Lunch: Grilled Chicken and Avocado Salad
- Dinner: Butternut Squash and Sage Risotto
- Dessert: Fig and Ricotta Toast

Day 7:
- Breakfast: Beet and Berry Liver Smoothie
- Lunch: Halibut in Herb Crust with Roasted Vegetables
- Dinner: Quinoa and Roasted Vegetable Salad
- Dessert: Baked Pears with Honey and Walnuts

Feel free to swap meals between days to suit your preferences or schedule. Enjoy your meals!

Chapter 10: Practical Tips for Healthy Eating

Simple Strategies for Long-Term Success

———— ❖ ————

Shopping Tips

Plan Before You Shop

Make a list: Start by planning your meals for the week. This helps you buy only what you need, avoid waste and save money.

Check for deals and coupons: Look out for sales, coupons and special offers. Many stores offer loyalty programs that can lead to significant savings.

Shop seasonally: Purchase fruits and vegetables that are in season. They're not only cheaper but also taste better.

Buy in bulk: For non-perishable items and staples such as rice, pasta and canned goods, it's advisable to buy in large quantities. However, be mindful of storage space and expiration dates.

While Shopping

Stick to your list: It's easy to be tempted by unnecessary items. Sticking to your list can help you manage your budget better.

Read labels: Pay attention to nutritional information and expiration dates. Choose healthier products with less added sugar and sodium.

Quality over quantity: Sometimes, it's worth paying a bit more for higher quality products that last longer or taste better.

Tips for Food Storage

Fruits and Vegetables

Separate ethylene producers and absorbers: Ethylene gas can accelerate ripening. Store ethylene-producing fruits like apples and bananas separately from ethylene-sensitive products like leafy vegetables.

Use your fridge wisely: Most vegetables keep well in the vegetable drawer of your fridge, which maintains a slightly different humidity level.

Meat and Fish

Freeze if not using immediately: If you're not going to use meat or fish within a couple of days, freeze it. Use airtight containers or freezer bags to prevent freezer burn.

Thaw safely: Always thaw frozen meat in the fridge or using the microwave's defrost setting, never at room temperature.

Dry Goods

Airtight containers: Store flour, sugar, cereals and other dry goods in airtight containers to keep them fresh longer and protect against pests.

Meal Preparation

Cook in Bulk

Cook in large batches: Prepare meals in large quantities and cook them. This saves time and energy. Portion out the meals and store them in the fridge or freezer.

Versatile ingredients: Cook versatile base ingredients in bulk, like rice, pasta or roasted vegetables. These can be used throughout the week in different dishes.

Efficient Time Use

Prepare once, eat twice: When cooking, make enough for leftovers. Many dishes like soups, stews and casseroles are great for this.

Prep ingredients in advance: Wash, chop and store vegetables and other ingredients in advance. This makes putting meals together much quicker.

Healthy Eating

Ensure variety: Try to include a variety of foods in your meals to ensure you're getting a range of nutrients.

Watch portions: Be mindful of portion sizes to avoid overeating. Using smaller plates can help control portions.

Smart shopping, effective food storage and efficient meal preparation can transform your eating habits, save you time and money and contribute to a healthier lifestyle. Implementing these tips can allow you to enjoy fresh, delicious meals that benefit both your well-being and your budget.

Strategies for Maintaining a Balanced Diet

A balanced diet is crucial for overall health and well-being. It involves consuming a variety of foods in the right proportions to achieve and maintain optimal health. This chapter introduces strategies to help individuals develop and maintain a balanced diet that supports their health goals.

Understand the Basics of Nutrition

To eat a balanced diet, it's important to understand the basics of nutrition. This includes knowledge about macronutrients (carbohydrates, proteins and fats) and micronutrients (vitamins and minerals). Each of these nutrients plays a specific role in the body and a balanced diet should include a healthy mix of all these nutrients. Carbohydrates provide energy for daily activities and should come from whole grains, fruits, vegetables and legumes.

Proteins are essential for building and repairing tissues and should be obtained from lean meat, poultry, fish, beans and nuts.

Fats are important for brain health and energy provision but should be consumed in moderation, with healthy sources such as avocados, nuts, seeds and olive oil being preferred.

Vitamins and minerals are crucial for various body functions, including supporting the immune system and bone health. A varied diet rich in fruits, vegetables and lean proteins typically provides a good mix of these nutrients.

Plan Your Meals

Meal planning is an effective tool for a balanced diet. It involves deciding what you will eat for the coming week and preparing meals in advance. This strategy can help you:

Avoid unhealthy choices: By planning, you reduce the likelihood of reaching for convenient but unhealthy options when hungry.

Ensure variety: Planning allows you to ensure you're incorporating a variety of foods into your diet that cover all necessary nutrients.

Control portions: Preparing your meals in advance allows you to control portion sizes and avoid overeating.

Practice Mindful Eating

Mindful eating is about being fully present during meals, paying attention to the taste, texture and sensations of the food. This practice can help you enjoy your meals more and recognize when you're full, reducing the risk of overeating. Tips for mindful eating include:
- Eating slowly and without distraction.
- Listening to the body's hunger and fullness signals.
- Appreciating the appearance and taste of your food.

Stay Hydrated

Water is essential for health but is often overlooked as part of a balanced diet. Adequate hydration helps regulate body temperature, maintain joint health and promote organ function. Adults should drink at least 8-8 glasses of water a day, more if they are active or in a hot climate.

Tailor Your Diet to Your Lifestyle

The body, lifestyle and nutritional needs differ from person to person. What's good for one may not be suitable for another. When planning your diet, consider factors like age, gender, activity level and health status. You can also consult a healthcare provider or a dietitian to tailor a diet plan to your specific needs.

Limit Processed Foods and Added Sugars

Processed foods and beverages high in added sugar can undermine your health goals. They often contain many calories and few nutrients. Aim to eat as many whole, unprocessed foods as possible. These include fruits, vegetables, whole grains, lean protein and healthy fats.

A balanced diet requires a combination of knowledge, planning and mindfulness. By understanding the basics of nutrition, planning meals, practicing mindful eating, staying hydrated, tailoring your diet to your lifestyle and limiting processed foods and added sugars, you can enhance your health and well-being. Remember, small, consistent changes over time can lead to significant, lasting benefits.

CONCLUSION

Your Next Steps Toward a Healthier You

———— ❖ ————

As we close the pages of the "Fatty Liver Cookbook", it's important to reflect on the journey we've embarked on together. This cookbook was designed not merely as a collection of recipes but as a guide to inspire you to change your eating and lifestyle habits for the benefit of your liver health.

Addressing and potentially reversing fatty liver disease requires more than just dietary changes; it necessitates a holistic approach to lifestyle modification. The recipes and tips included in this book serve as a springboard to a healthier, more vibrant life. By choosing nutrient-rich, liver-friendly foods, you're taking significant steps to lessen the burden on your liver, allowing it to heal and function more effectively.

Remember, the path to better health is not a race but a marathon. Changes in liver health occur gradually and consistency is key. Integrate the principles and recipes from this cookbook into your daily routine and tailor them to your personal taste and nutritional needs. This personalized approach ensures that the journey is not only beneficial but also enjoyable and sustainable in the long term.

It's also important to complement your dietary habits with other healthy lifestyle practices such as regular physical activity, adequate hydration and sufficient sleep. These behaviors work together to improve your overall health and well-being and support the healing process of your liver.

We hope you will continue to explore and experiment with the recipes in this cookbook. Make your kitchen a place of creativity, joy and healing. Share your culinary creations with your loved ones and let your journey inspire them to embark on their own path to liver health.

In conclusion, we hope the "Fatty Liver Cookbook" has equipped you with the knowledge, tools and inspiration you need to make positive changes in your life. Remember, every meal is an opportunity to nourish your body and support the health of your liver. We feel honored to have been part of your journey and wish you continued success and well-being on your path.

Thank you for choosing to take this important step toward a healthier future. May the recipes and guidance in this book continue to serve you well, bringing not only healing but also pleasure and satisfaction to your table. Here's to a healthier liver and a happier life!

BONUS

Additional Tools to Support Your Liver-Friendly Lifestyle

———— ❖ ————

Welcome to the bonus page!

Here you can download **"Customizable Weekly Meal Plans"**, an unmissable management and motivational ebook that will accompany you on your fatty liver diet journey.

Download it now!

SCAN THIS QR-CODE TO DOWNLOAD YOUR GREAT BONUS INSTANTLY!

IF YOU APPRECIATED THE BOOK, YOU CAN LEAVE AN HONEST REVIEW ON AMAZON HERE!

Made in the USA
Monee, IL
12 February 2025

12149162R00059